NORTH AMERICAN FIELD GUIDES

EDIBLE WILD PLANTS

Douglas W. Darnowski

Field Guides

An Imprint of Abdo Reference | abdobooks.com

CONTENTS

Herbs and Spices

Nuts and Seeds

Roots, Tubers, and Bulbs

Seaweeds

SAFETY—Always find and eat edible wild plants with a trusted adult. Do not collect or taste any plants without an adult's permission. Be sure you are eating the correct plant; if you have any doubt, do not eat it. Do not collect plants in polluted areas, along roadways, or on private property. Also note the possibility of food allergies—any new food could cause harmful reactions. One way to check is to rub a little of the new plant food on the tip of your tongue. If it starts to tingle, that could be an allergy, so be careful and stop eating that plant food. Many wild edible plants contain substances that may bother a few people—be careful! For example, many people today are allergic to latex, which is found in a number of plants, including wild lettuce and yellow lotus, both found in this field guide.

WHAT ARE EDIBLE PLANTS?

Some plants grow in the wild, not in gardens. They are edible when you can eat them safely, without being harmed. They are good for you because they are full of vitamins, minerals, and flavor. It is a great adventure to find food in wild places. But do not remove them from places that prohibit plant removal, such as some state or national parks.

Wild edible plants can be eaten in several ways. Many of them have tasty stems and leaves that you can add to salads or soups. Others have sweet, colorful fruits that form after they flower, and many others can be used as spices to give extra flavor. In the kitchen, cooks often have a jar of allspice from the tropics for adding to pumpkin bread and muffins, but spicebush berries from the woods can be ground up and used in the same way. Some wild plants drop delicious nuts in the fall. Others have storage organs, such as wild potatoes, that are crunchy, full of starch, and can be roasted and gobbled up with salt and butter.

Why do these plants have edible parts? Some are not meant to be eaten, but they taste good and are safe to eat. Others are naturally meant to be eaten, such as fruits. When fruits are eaten by wildlife, it guarantees that the seeds are spread all over, giving the plants a wider range of places to grow.

All of these parts are nutritious. Some plants have plenty of nitrogen, which the body needs to make strong muscles. Others are rich in calcium, to help bones grow well. The chlorophyll in green plant parts is very much like the heme in blood. This compound carries oxygen from the lungs to the body's cells. Chlorophyll can be used by the body to make that heme.

Imagine how great it will feel to find your own foods and to be a real explorer. You can do that really close to home, as you will learn in this book. And you will learn to try new foods, which is part of growing up and living a full life.

WHAT ARE WILD PLANTS?

Wild plants grow without help from humans. They simply grow where their seeds find the right amounts of light and water. The other way that plants grow near us is if we cultivate them, or grow them on purpose. We do that in gardens or on farms.

There are two kinds of wild plants. Wild native plants have always grown in North America and still grow there today. We harvest them where we find them. The other wild plants have been brought from another place, such as Asia, where they grew originally. They now also grow in North America where they find the right growing conditions. This book includes both wild native plants and wild introduced plants. Both of these provide sources of delicious and nutritious food.

BE SAFE

When looking for edible wild plants, it is very important to be safe at all times. Review the safety message on page 3 of this book before collecting or eating any wild plants.

Wild things are wonderful, but they are not always as clean as they should be. We are used to eating foods from the grocery store. This food has been raised for cleanliness and is usually washed before we buy it. Our stomachs are not ready for a little dirt, unlike the stomachs of our ancestors who were more used to eating wild foods. So be sure to take wild foods from unpolluted, clean places only. Do not collect any plants with animal waste on or near them. And thoroughly wash anything you intend to eat fresh or cooked.

HOW TO USE THIS BOOK

Tab shows the edible plant category.

The edible plant's common name appears here.

FRUITS

AMERICAN BARBERRY

(BERBERIS CANADENSIS)

These small, thorny bushes spread by underground stems ...rm clumps of plants. In fall, the American barberry ...uces shiny, oval red berries that are rich in vitamin C. ... tart flavor makes them great for making juice and ...s. The plants are popular for their beautiful color and ...e, so they can be found in many gardens. Extracts from ... plant are good for heart and brain health.

This paragraph provides information about the edible plant.

HOW TO SPOT

Size: 3 to 7 feet (0.9 to 2.1 m) tall
Habitat: Widely varied, including woods and fields
Fruit: 0.3 inches (7.6 mm) long
Leaves: 0.5 to 1.5 inches (1.3 to 3.8 cm) long
Range: Eastern United States and Canada

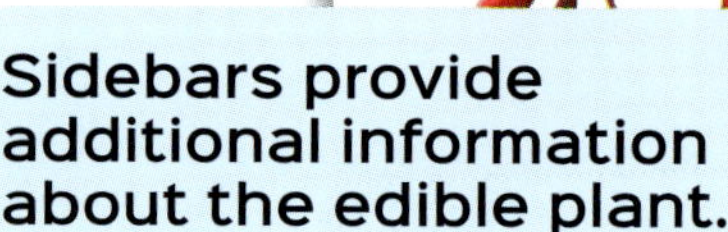

Sidebars provide additional information about the edible plant.

TYPES OF FRUITS

Fruits are grouped by how they are built. Simple fruits (blueberries) come from the inner parts of one flower. Accessory fruits (strawberries) include other flower parts. Aggregate fruits (blackberries) are from bunches of inner flower parts. Multiple fruits (pineapples) are from many flowers stuck together.

10

IERICAN ELDERBERRY

MBUCUS CANADENSIS)

rican elderberry trees appear in open lots that are
ming woodlands as well as on the edge of forests. Their
ns have no thorns, which helps distinguish them from a
-alike, the devil's walking stick. In summer, the trees make
ups of umbrella-shaped, sweet-smelling white flowers.
dark purple-black berries are used to make juice and jelly,
ch can kill viruses in the human body. These superfruits
tain antioxidants and may provide health benefits. Be
e to cook them because unripe or raw berries, as well as
stem, root, seeds, and leaves, are toxic.

FUN FACT

The American elderberry has a close cousin also found in North America, European elderberry. It forms a wide clump of short stems with many long leaves.

HOW TO SPOT

Size: 12 to 20 feet (3.7 to 6.1 m) tall
Habitat: Streams, moist forests, disturbed areas
Fruit: 0.1 to 0.3 inches (0.3 to 0.8 cm) long
Leaves: Compound, 6 to 10 inches (15.2 to 25.4 cm) long
Range: United States east of the Mississippi River and the eastern half of Canada

11

The edible plant's scientific name appears here.

***Fun Facts* give interesting information about the edible plant.**

Images show the edible plant.

***How to Spot* features give information about the edible plant's size, habitat, flowers, and range.**

DOG VIOLET *(VIOLA LABRIDORICA)*

A common perennial in eastern North America, dog violets often grow in lawns. Heart-shaped leaves come from the base of the plant. These violets grow mixed among the grass and along the edges of gardens. In the spring, they make bright purple flowers, varying in intensity, or white flowers with purple lines or blotches. The flowers can add a dash of bright color to salads, or they can be sprinkled on top of cooked vegetables. Don't cook the violets themselves if you want maximum color.

HOW TO SPOT

Size: 6 to 10 inches (15.2 to 25.4 cm) tall
Habitat: Rich, moist soils, and lawns
Flowers: 0.8 inches (2 cm) wide
Leaves: 3 to 6 inches (7.6 to 15.2 cm) long
Range: Central and eastern United States, central and eastern Canada, and eastern Mexico

FUN FACT

Dog violets can be used as a source of dye for coloring cloth. The fresh flowers are mashed up and applied to the cloth, which will turn gray or green depending on what other chemicals are added.

WHITE WATER LILY

(NYMPHAEA ODORATA)

Round leaves and white flowers of this delicious perennial plant float on the surface of ponds and lakes. Bees drink the sweet nectar and eat the yellow pollen, and people love the strong, sweet odor of its flowers in summer. The flowers are white with yellow centers due to their stamens. The stems are hidden in the mud at the bottoms of ponds, so they are normally hard to see. Add the raw flowers or petals to a salad or sprinkle over other dishes as a garnish.

HOW TO SPOT

Size: 3 to 4 feet (0.9 to 1.2 m) tall
Habitat: Ponds, lakes, and slow-flowing streams
Flowers: 3 to 6 inches (7.6 to 15.2 cm) wide
Leaves: Up to 8 inches (20.3 cm) wide
Range: United States, Canada, and northern Mexico

FLOWERS AS SALAD ACCENTS

Flowers can make a big difference in a salad. Sprinkling edible flowers on a green salad makes it come to life. New flavors are added.

AMERICAN BARBERRY

(BERBERIS CANADENSIS)

These small, thorny bushes spread by underground stems to form clumps of plants. In fall, the American barberry produces shiny, oval red berries that are rich in vitamin C. Their tart flavor makes them great for making juice and jellies. The plants are popular for their beautiful color and shape, so they can be found in many gardens.

HOW TO SPOT

Size: 3 to 7 feet (0.9 to 2.1 m) tall
Habitat: Widely varied, including woods and fields
Fruit: 0.3 inches (7.6 mm) long
Leaves: 0.5 to 1.5 inches (1.3 to 3.8 cm) long
Range: Eastern United States and Canada

TYPES OF FRUITS

Fruits are grouped by how they are built. Simple fruits (blueberries) come from the inner parts of one flower. Accessory fruits (strawberries) include other flower parts. Aggregate fruits (blackberries) are from bunches of inner flower parts. Multiple fruits (pineapples) are from many flowers stuck together.

AMERICAN ELDERBERRY

(SAMBUCUS CANADENSIS)

American elderberry trees appear in open lots that are becoming woodlands as well as on the edge of forests. Their stems have no thorns, which helps distinguish them from a look-alike, the devil's walking stick. In summer, the trees make groups of umbrella-shaped, sweet-smelling white flowers. The dark purple-black berries are used to make juice and jelly. These superfruits contain antioxidants. Be sure to cook them because unripe or raw berries, as well as the stem, root, seeds, and leaves, are toxic.

FUN FACT

The American elderberry has a close cousin also found in North America, European elderberry. It forms a wide clump of short stems with many long leaves.

HOW TO SPOT

Size: 12 to 20 feet (3.7 to 6.1 m) tall
Habitat: Streams, moist forests, disturbed areas
Fruit: 0.1 to 0.3 inches (0.3 to 0.8 cm) long
Leaves: Compound, 6 to 10 inches (15.2 to 25.4 cm) long
Range: United States east of the Mississippi River and the eastern half of Canada

AMERICAN GOOSEBERRY

(RIBES HIRTELLUM)

American gooseberry bushes usually grow in the open, but sometimes they grow in the woods. They have thorny spines on their stems. The leaves have three to five lobes. This bush makes green flowers in the spring. The pink-red berries that follow are worth the work of picking for their sweet flavor. These fruits can be eaten fresh, used to make jelly, or added to cereal. Their flavor is similar to the blueberry.

HOW TO SPOT

Size: 2 to 5 feet (0.6 to 1.5 m) tall
Habitat: Rich, moist soils
Fruit: 0.25 to 0.33 inches (0.6 to 0.8 cm) wide
Leaves: 1 to 2.5 inches (2.5 to 6.4 cm) long
Range: Northern and eastern United States and Canada, except British Columbia

FUN FACT

Gooseberries provide lots of vitamin C and vitamin A. Vitamin C helps grow healthy hair and skin. Vitamin A promotes eye health.

AMERICAN MOUNTAIN ASH

(SORBUS AMERICANA)

This small tree is related to roses and apples. It makes white, flat, umbrella-shaped clusters of flowers in the spring. The tree bears clusters of orange berries. These small berries have tiny flaps of leaf-like tissue at one end. They grow in large groups, ripening in the autumn. The sweet-tasting fruit has a pleasant bitterness and should be frozen or cooked to reduce the bitterness and improve edibility. American mountain ash fruit is popular for pies and jellies.

HOW TO SPOT

Size: A tree up to 35 feet (10.7 m) tall
Habitat: Moist, rich woods
Fruit: 0.1 to 0.2 inches (0.3 to 0.5 cm) wide
Leaves: Compound, 6 to 10 inches (15.2 to 25.4 cm) long
Range: Eastern United States and Canada

AMERICAN PERSIMMON

(DIOSPYROS VIRGINIANA)

An American persimmon tree has shiny oval leaves and makes white to yellow flowers in the spring. The tree's shiny orange fruit is sweet and sticky after a frost. Before frost, it is hard, partly green, and very astringent. So wait until after frost to eat it. It can be made into jams and jellies, baked into cakes and breads, or preserved as a pulp after the seeds and skin are removed. The fruits are often easiest to harvest by picking them up after they fall to the ground.

HOW TO SPOT

Size: Up to 80 to 100 feet (24.4 to 30.5 m) tall
Habitat: Well-drained, rich woodland soils
Fruit: 0.8 to 2.3 inches (2 to 5.8 cm) wide
Leaves: 2 to 6 inches long (5.1 to 15.2 cm)
Range: United States east of the Mississippi River and Canada (Ontario)

FUN FACT

The bark of the American persimmon is very unique. It has lines running up and down that divide the thick, gray bark into irregular squares. This makes it easy to identify the tree.

AMERICAN PLUM *(PRUNUS AMERICANA)*

This small perennial tree prefers coarse, sandy soils of low to moderate fertility. It is remarkably hardy, surviving in temperatures as low as –40°F (–40°C). Watch for the easy-to-spot trees with pointed oval leaves. The trees are covered in small white flowers in spring. If you return to the tree in summer, you may find a delicious harvest. The fruits can be yellow, pink, red, or purple. While the skin is tart, the flesh of the fruit is sweet, soft, and rich in flavor.

HOW TO SPOT

Size: 10 to 20 feet (3 to 6.1 m) tall

Habitat: Open and semi-open fields, poorer soils

Fruit: 1 inch (2.5 cm) wide

Leaves: 2 to 4 inches (5.1 to 10.2 cm) long

Range: Eastern half of North America

ANTIOXIDANTS FROM FRUIT AND YOUR HEALTH

Bright colors in plant foods are a sign of antioxidants. These chemicals help protect the body's cells from free radicals, which are formed from the oxidation process. So go ahead and eat blueberries and strawberries.

ARROWWOOD VIBURNUM

(VIBURNUM DENTATUM)

These woodland bushes have oval leaves that are toothed on the edges. The plants bear many dark purple-black berries containing a thin flesh around one large seed per fruit. The flesh can be processed into jams, jellies, and sauces.

HOW TO SPOT

Size: 3 to 10 feet (0.9 to 3 m) tall, spreading up to 10 feet (3 m) wide

Habitat: Fertile, well-watered woodlands

Fruit: 0.2 to 0.3 inches (0.5 to 0.8 cm) wide

Leaves: 1.5 to 4 inches (3.8 to 10.2 cm) long

Range: Eastern half of North America

FUN FACT

Arrowwood viburnum gets its name from its use by American Indians for the shafts of their arrows. The stems were straight and durable, and could easily be made into arrows.

BEARBERRY *(ARCTOSTAPHYLOS UVA-URSI)*

Bearberry got its name from the fact that bears like to eat it. This small shrub grows in cold, northern regions of North America and at higher altitudes farther south. In summer, it makes small clusters of bell-shaped, pink flowers. The red berry fruits are tart, like unsweetened cranberries. The plants can be found year-round because of their dark, oval, shiny, evergreen leaves. Some Amerian Indians dried and smoked the leaves in place of tobacco.

HOW TO SPOT

Size: 6 to 12 inches (15.2 to 30.5 cm tall) and spreading up to 6 feet (1.8 m) along the surface of the ground by long branches

Habitat: Well-drained (sandy or gravelly) soils in northern boreal forests

Fruit: 0.3 to 0.5 inch (0.8 to 1.3 cm) wide

Leaves: 1 inch (2.5 cm) long

Range: United States south to Virginia, Illinois, Nebraska, and in the mountains from New Mexico to Alaska, and Canada

FRUITS

BEAUTYBERRY *(CALLICARPA AMERICANA)*

American beautyberry shrubs grow near woodlands in the eastern United States, as well as in many gardens. This plant has elliptical to oval, medium green leaves that are hairy underneath. The shrubs make long clusters of white flowers in the summer. People enjoy this plant's shiny purple berries, cutting them for decorations in the fall and winter. Birds eat many of the berries. Beautyberries are astringent, so they should be cooked before they are made into jellies and wines.

HOW TO SPOT

Size: 5 to 8 feet (1.5 to 2.4 m) tall
Habitat: Open areas with abundant rainfall; edges of woods
Fruit: 0.1 inch (0.3 cm) long
Leaves: 6 inches (15.2 cm) long
Range: Southeastern United States and northern Mexico

BLACK CHOKECHERRY

(PRUNUS VIRGINIANA)

The black chokecherry is a shrub or small tree. The leaves are oval with toothed edges. This plant makes chains of white flowers in the spring. It is in the same genus as cherries, with sweet dark purple-black fruit. The one seed per fruit is large compared to the total fruit size, so be careful not to bite down hard. The fruits are astringent, so they are usually cooked and made into jams, jellies, and wines. Only eat the fruit; any other part of the plant can be mildly toxic.

HOW TO SPOT

Size: 20 to 30 feet (6.1 to 9.1 m) tall; 18 to 25 feet (5.5 to 7.6 m) wide
Habitat: Rich, moist woodland edges with full sun
Fruit: 0.3 to 0.5 inches (0.8 to 1.3 cm) wide
Leaves: 1 to 4 inches (2.5 to 10.2 cm) long
Range: United States and Canada

BLACK HUCKLEBERRY

(GAYLUSSACIA BACCATA)

Black huckleberry bushes grow well in some shade in cool eastern woodlands in the United States and Canada. The bushes have elliptical leaves with toothed edges. In the spring, notice its bell-shaped pink flowers. This plant is a close relative of blueberries, though its fruits are a dark blue-black rather than the brighter blue of its cousin. The fruits can be used just like blueberries: eaten fresh, used in baked goods such as muffins, or turned into jams and jellies.

HOW TO SPOT

Size: 1 to 3 feet (0.3 to 0.9 m) tall, occasionally shorter
Habitat: Moist woodland soils in cooler areas
Fruit: 0.2 inches (0.5 cm) wide
Leaves: Up to 2 inches (5.1 cm) long
Range: Eastern North America

FUN FACT

Black huckleberry should not be confused with garden huckleberry. Garden huckleberry is a fruit from the same family as tomato and potato.

COMMON BLACKBERRY

(RUBUS ALLEGHENIENSIS)

Common blackberry bushes thrive in open, sunny ground, with their graceful canes arching up from the ground. The canes grow one year, flowering white the next summer. This plant has compound leaves made of three to five leaflets, with many prickles. The stems are covered in thorns. The purple-black berries are sweet and soft, having passed from green to red to purple. The berries are made into pies and cobblers, as well as wine, jams, and jellies.

FUN FACT

You can dye cloth with blackberries. Cook the blackberries to release all of their color. The cloth will turn blue or purple.

HOW TO SPOT

Size: 5 to 8 feet (1.5 to 2.4 m) long canes that bend back toward the ground
Habitat: Open ground, often recently cleared
Fruit: 0.5 to 1 inch (1.3 to 2.5 cm) long
Leaves: Compound, 2.5 to 4 inches (6.4 to 10.2 cm) long
Range: Eastern North America

FRUITS

EASTERN PRICKLY PEAR CACTUS

(OPUNTIA HUMIFUSA)

This cactus looks like a large clump of round, flat green-gray pads covered in spines. Its bright yellow flowers appear in spring or summer. Small pear-shaped, reddish fruits form after the flowers are pollinated. The fruit contains a red-pink flesh and many round seeds. The flesh can be eaten fresh or extracted and used to make jam or jelly. The stems, cleaned of their spines, can also be eaten. They are known in Spanish as *nopal* or *nopales*.

HOW TO SPOT

Size: 6 to 18 inches (15.2 to 45.7 cm) tall
Habitat: Dry, rocky, sunny areas with poor soils
Fruit: 1.2 to 2 inches (3 to 5.1 cm) long; 0.5 to 0.8 inches (1.3 to 2 cm) wide
Range: North America, except the West Coast

GOLDEN CURRANT *(RIBES AUREUM)*

The leaves of the golden currant are lobed like goose feet. These bushes erupt with yellow flowers in spring, followed by purple-black berries. The fruits can be eaten fresh. They need sugar to make them really tasty. When made into jam or jelly, their golden color and sweet flavor can be enjoyed on toast all year. These are native in the western part of North America, but they now also grow in the east.

Size: 3 to 10 feet (0.9 to 3 m) tall
Habitat: Moist woodlands
Fruit: 0.3 to 0.5 inch (0.8 to 1.3 cm) wide
Leaves: 0.5 to 2 inches (1.3 to 5.1 cm) wide
Range: Most of North America

HAWTHORN *(CRATAEGUS DOUGLASII)*

This shrub prefers the hills in Canada and northwestern United States. It has fan-shaped leaves with toothed edges. Its thorns are up to 1 inch (2.5 cm) long. The fruits are a blackish-purple color and look like small plums. They follow the spring bloom of cup-shaped white flowers. They can be eaten fresh or used in various cooked dishes, such as jams and jellies. Growing in the western part of North America, where wildfires are common, this shrub is able to recover quickly when burned.

HOW TO SPOT

Size: 25 to 30 feet (7.6 to 9.1 m) tall
Habitat: Forests 2,000 to 4,000 feet (609.6 to 1,219.2 m) in elevation
Fruit: 0.4 inch (1 cm) wide
Leaves: 2 to 3 inches (5.1 to 7.6 cm) long
Range: Canada and northwestern United States

FUN FACT
In Mexico, the Christmas drink *ponche* is made from the fruits of a hawthorn called *tejocote*.

HONEY MESQUITE

(PROSOPIS GLANDULOSA)

This small tree comes from dry areas. This member of the bean family thrives where water is hard to find. Its spring-blooming flowers are yellow, in clusters 2 to 3 inches (5.1 to 7.6 cm) long. The twisted seed pods resemble large flat pods from common beans. They can be dried and ground to make what is called mesquite meal or mesquite flour. This can be used in baking. Mesquite flour adds a caramel flavor to dishes.

HOW TO SPOT

Size: 20 to 30 feet (6.1 to 9.1 m) tall
Habitat: Dry desert or semidesert soils
Fruit: Up to 8 inches (20.3 cm) long
Leaves: Compound, 3 to 6 inches (7.6 to 15.2 cm) long
Range: Southwestern United States and northern Mexico

LOWBUSH BLUEBERRY

(VACCINIUM ANGUSTIFOLIUM)

These short bushes are a favorite source of sweet berries. They spread by underground rhizomes in open, sunny fields. In the spring, white or pink bell-shaped flowers cover the branches. Later, the bright blueberries can be collected and eaten fresh or used in jams, jellies, juices, and baked goods. They are gathered using special cup-shaped rakes. The leaves turn a beautiful fire red in the autumn.

HOW TO SPOT

Size: 6 to 24 inches (15.2 to 61 cm) tall

Habitat: Moist, acidic soils in cooler areas or higher elevations

Fruit: 0.1 to 0.2 inches (0.3 to 0.5 cm) wide

Leaves: 0.8 to 1.5 inches (2 to 3.8 cm) long

Range: Northeastern North America

MAYPOP *(PASSIFLORA INCARNATA)*

Maypop is the most northern of the many species of passion fruits. Most grow in tropical and subtropical places such as Central and South America. The vines have five-lobed leaves. The bright purple flowers, with their ring of purple filaments, are followed by yellow oval fruits that fall off the vines when ripe. These contain black seeds surrounded by sweet, tropical-flavored yellow juice. The juice is good for making punch and jelly and for flavoring baked goods.

HOW TO SPOT

Size: Vines up to 25 feet (7.6 m) long
Habitat: Rich, moist soils
Fruit: 4 inches (10.2 cm) long
Leaves: 2.5 to 6 inches (6.4 to 15.2 cm) wide
Range: Southeastern United States

FUN FACT

Maypop gets its name from how late it begins to grow each year. It comes up from deep underground. Often, you think that it has died, and then it "pops" up out of the ground in May.

MOCK STRAWBERRY

(POTENTILLA INDICA)

Looking like a typical strawberry plant, to which it is related, mock strawberry prefers fertile ground. This plant's leaves are made of three leaflets that are rounded with a toothed edge. In the spring and summer, it makes yellow flowers. When pollinated, the flowers produce red fruit. This fruit is rounder than true strawberries and smaller, covered in seeds. The fruits are edible, though less flavorful than true strawberries. The fruits can be eaten fresh or used in other foods. They can be made into jams, jellies, and sauces.

HOW TO SPOT

Size: 4 inches (10.2 cm) tall, usually in larger patches 1 to 2 feet (0.3 to 0.6 m) in diameter

Habitat: Moist, rich soil, usually in full sun

Fruit: 0.5 inches (1.3 cm) wide

Leaves: Compound, 0.5 to 2 inches (1.3 to 5.1 cm)

Range: Eastern half of North America and the West Coast

FUN FACT

Mock strawberry can be cultivated like true strawberries. Just look for them in lawns, dig them up (with permission and with roots), and plant them in full sun, giving lots of water.

MULBERRY *(MORUS NIGRA)*

This tree species with shiny leaves came from Asia, where it is still grown for its dark purple-black fruit. In spring, the tree makes small white-and-green flowers that turn into the fruits. They are a favorite food of wildlife, so they will have to be picked quickly. These trees grow wild in many places, even in developed cities.

FUN FACT

Mulberry trees were first introduced to North America in an attempt to raise silk worm moths, which provide the thread to make silk cloth. This did not work. However, this has left us with delicious free fruit.

HOW TO SPOT

Size: Up to 35 feet (10.7 m) tall; 45 feet (13.7 m) wide
Habitat: Sunny, well-drained soils
Fruit: 1 to 2 inches (2.5 to 5.1 cm) long
Leaves: 4 to 8 inches (10.2 to 20.3 cm) wide; 6 to 10 inches (15.2 to 25.4 cm) long
Range: Eastern United States and Canada

MUSCADINE GRAPE

(VITIS ROTUNDIFOLIA)

Muscadine grape vines twist and rope around trees and fences in the American southeast. The heart-shaped leaves have toothed edges. The flowers are tiny and yellow green. They grow in clusters in the spring. This native grape has red or bronze fruit that makes delectable juice, pies, and wine. The skin of the grape is thick and tart, with sweet flesh inside.

HOW TO SPOT

Size: 8 to 12 feet (2.4 to 3.7 m) long; 6 to 8 feet (1.8 to 2.4 m) wide
Habitat: Disturbed ground such as roadsides, dry upland forests, swamps
Fruit: 0.5 to 1 inch (1.3 to 2.5 cm) wide
Leaves: 4 by 4 inches (10.2 by 10.2 cm)
Range: Southeastern United States

NORTHERN CRANBERRY

(VACCINIUM OXYCOCCOS)

The cranberry bush thrives in moist, acidic soils with lots of sun. The first colonists in New England ate these tart, red berries. The low-growing plant has lance-shaped leaves. The flowers, which are pink to white, are bell-shaped and hang down on the plant in spring. The red fruit, which is easy to dry for use in the winter, provides a wealth of vitamin C. This species is not the cranberry usually eaten at Thanksgiving dinner, being much shorter and with smaller fruit.

HOW TO SPOT

Size: 4 to 16 inches (10.2 to 40.6 cm) tall, creeping along the ground for 2 to 3 feet (0.6 to 0.9 m)
Habitat: Moist to wet soils, acidic, rich in dead plant material
Fruit: 0.5 inches (1.3 cm) wide
Leaves: Up to 0.4 inch (1 cm) long
Range: Canada and the northern United States

FUN FACT

Cranberries are in the heath family, the same family as blueberries and huckleberries. These berries are similar, all with bright colors.

OREGON GRAPE *(MAHONIA AQUIFOLIUM)*

A relative of the barberry, the Oregon grape is not a grape. But its blue-black fruits look a lot like grapes. This bush has compound leaves made up of spiny leaflets. After the yellow flowers bloom in clusters in the spring on this bush, the fruit follows. Their sour flavor is excellent in jams and jellies. The juice can be mixed with that of other fruits, such as grape juice, to make a delicious fruit juice cocktail.

FUN FACT

The Oregon grape is widely grown for its beautiful springtime flowers. It can sometimes be found in shadier spots in gardens.

HOW TO SPOT

Size: 3 to 10 feet (0.9 to 3 m) tall; up to 5 feet (1.5 m) wide
Habitat: Forests with moist, rich soils
Fruit: 0.3 to 0.5 inches (0.8 to 1.3 cm) wide
Leaves: Compound, up to 12 inches (30.5 cm) long
Range: Western and parts of eastern North America and Canada (Ontario)

PARTRIDGEBERRY

(MITCHELLA REPENS)

Partridgeberry plants dot the woods of eastern North America, producing bright red fruit on their creeping stems. Partridgeberry plants stand out against the brown leaf litter on the forest floor. They have shiny, dark evergreen leaves that are oval to heart-shaped. Each fruit is actually the result of two flowers, which bloom white in the spring and summer, linked together at their bases. The flavor of these twin red berries is very mild, with a hint of wintergreen.

HOW TO SPOT

Size: Up to 2.5 inches (6.4 cm) tall; up to 4 feet (1.2 m) wide

Habitat: Dry or moist woodlands, with fertile soil

Fruit: 0.3 inches (0.8 cm) wide

Leaves: 0.8 inches (2 cm) long; 0.5 inches (1.3 cm) wide

Range: Eastern North America

PAWPAW *(ASIMINA TRILOBA)*

Pawpaw trees, with their smooth gray bark, are easy to identify from their large, oval leaves that smell like gasoline. However, the fruits are delicious. Although it is the northernmost member of a family of mostly tropical fruits, the pawpaw lives in shady woods. The red-brown flowers with three petals bloom in the spring. This tree's yellow-green fruit tastes like a combination of pineapple, mango, and banana, with a soft, custard texture. You have to be quick to pick the ripe fruits. They are favorites of opossums and raccoons.

HOW TO SPOT

Size: Trees up to 35 feet (10.7 m) tall
Habitat: Moist rich woodlands, usually near water
Fruit: 2 to 6 inches (5.1 to 15.2 cm) long; 1 to 3 inches (2.5 to 7.6 cm) wide
Leaves: 6 to 12 inches (15.2 to 30.5 cm) long
Range: Eastern North America (except Florida)

FUN FACT

Be careful! Pawpaws are delicious, but they contain seeds that should not be eaten. The seeds are very large and dark, so they are easy to spot and take out.

SASKATOON SERVICEBERRY

(AMELANCHIER ALNIFOLIA)

These small, multibranched trees enjoy shade, either under forest trees or in canyons. New small trees form from suckers of older trees, so they grow in colonies of plants. They have oval to circular leaves with toothed edges. In the spring, the tree is full of white flowers, like those of an apple tree. Their small, round purple fruits taste like a mix of blueberry and apple. The fruits can be used in similar ways to blueberries, for jams and jellies, in baked goods, and for eating fresh.

HOW TO SPOT

Size: 3 to 18 feet (0.9 to 5.5 m)
Habitat: Canyons, forest under the trees
Fruit: 0.3 to 0.6 inches (0.8 to 1.5 cm) wide
Leaves: 0.8 to 2 inches (2 to 5.1 cm) long; 0.5 to 1.8 inches (1.3 to 4.6 cm) wide
Range: Western North America and Canada (Ontario and Quebec)

SEA BUCKTHORN

(HIPPOPHAE RHAMNOIDES)

Sea buckthorn is a small tree or large bush. It has narrow gray-green leaves on spiny stems. It is very cold hardy. The bright orange berries can be made into delicious juice or jelly. Sea buckthorn tea is also very tasty and rich in vitamins C, E, and B12, as well as carotene. This plant is widely grown in Europe, where it is native, and in some places in cooler areas of North America.

FUN FACT

Sea buckthorn juice has a mix of sour and sweet flavors, something like pineapple.

HOW TO SPOT

Size: 7 to 13 feet (2.1 to 4 m) tall
Habitat: Dry soils in cold climates
Fruit: 0.2 to 0.3 inches (0.5 to 0.8 cm)
Leaves: 1 to 3 inches (2.5 to 7.6 cm) long
Range: United States (Colorado and Ohio) and Canada (Alberta and Saskatchewan)

STRAWBERRY TOMATO

(PHYSALIS GRISEA)

The annual strawberry tomato is also called a ground-cherry. It is a spreading plant that has bright green leaves with pointed tips and curved edges. It is a relative of potatoes, tomatoes, and tomatillos. Its pineapple flavor is a favorite for pies, jams, and jellies, as well as for fresh eating. This plant's long, green-yellow flowers bloom in spring and summer. Its orange fruits are covered in dried, papery leaves, like a little package. The fruits form inside.

HOW TO SPOT

Size: Up to 18 inches (45.7 cm) tall, often spreading across the ground

Habitat: Pastures, roadsides, and other cleared places

Fruit: 0.5 to 0.8 inches (1.3 to 2 cm) wide

Leaves: 2 to 3 inches (5.1 to 7.6 cm) long

Range: Eastern United States and West Coast

THIMBLEBERRY *(RUBUS PARVIFLORUS)*

Thimbleberries are related to raspberries and blackberries but have fruits that are wider and lighter colored. These berries are made of many small juice sacs arranged in a dome. This tart, pink fruit can be used to make jams, jellies, and pies, when sweetened. They can also be used in a long-lasting American Indian food called pemmican, combining meat and fruit. Unlike its relatives, thimbleberry lacks sharp prickles. The stems are biennial, sprouting one year, fruiting the next, and then dying.

HOW TO SPOT

Size: 2 to 8 feet (0.6 to 2.4 m) tall
Habitat: Forests and mountains, usually in shady, cool areas with moist soils; along roads and railroads
Fruit: 0.5 inches (1.3 cm) wide
Leaves: Compound, up to 8 inches (20.3 cm) long
Range: Northern and western United States and Canada

FUN FACT

Thimbleberries have a hollow core. This makes the berries easy to fit on the tip of a finger, just like a thimble.

TRIFOLIATE ORANGE

(CITRUS TRIFOLIATA)

This relative of oranges and lemons is the hardiest member of its family. The tree has compound leaves with three leaflets. These leaves have a pleasant citrus smell because of the oil held in its leaves. The stems grow thorns up to 3 inches (7.6 cm) long. The unscented white flowers bloom in spring. The orange fruits are sour and bitter. Adding baking soda to the juice removes the bitterness, allowing the juice to be used to make jelly or marmalade.

FUN FACT

All citrus leaves have oil glands, from which their smell comes. Pick a leaf (watch out for the thorns!) and hold it up to the light. The clear spots in the leaf are the oil glands.

HOW TO SPOT

Size: 12 to 24 feet (3.7 to 7.3 m) tall
Habitat: Fertile moist soils in full sun
Fruit: 1.3 to 1.5 inches (3.3 to 3.8 cm) wide
Leaves: Compound, 1 to 2 inches (2.5 to 5.1 cm) wide; 1 to 2 inches (2.5 to 5.1 cm) long
Range: Eastern United States (except New England)

WILD STRAWBERRY *(FRAGARIA VESCA)*

This wild perennial relative of the strawberries grown in gardens produces smaller fruits. This plant has compound leaves made of three leaflets. The plant makes white flowers in the spring/summer. The delicious bright red fruits can be used in pies or baked goods, eaten fresh, or made into jam or jelly. They are covered in small seeds, like garden strawberries. Strawberry is part of the rose family, along with apple, peach, plum, and cherry.

FUN FACT

Wild strawberries are much sweeter than mock strawberries, and they are pointier, not round.

HOW TO SPOT

Size: 3 to 9 inches (7.6 to 22.9 cm) tall; 9 to 12 inches (22.9 to 30.5 cm) wide, in groups

Habitat: Fertile, moist, well-drained soils in full sun

Fruit: 1 to 1.5 inches (2.5 to 3.8 cm) long; 0.8 to 1 inch (2 to 2.5 cm) wide

Leaves: Compound, 3 to 6 inches (7.6 to 15.2 cm) long

Range: United States and Canada (except Nevada and the Yukon)

WRINKLED ROSE *(ROSA RUGOSA)*

The wrinkled rose loves bright sun and poor soils. This bush is easy to find on North America's beaches. It has compound leaves made of five to nine leaflets that have deep wrinkles. The deep pink flowers are followed by cherry-red fruits, called hips, rich in vitamin C. The hips can be made into jams and jellies, dried for including in tea mixes, and used in baked goods. They are also a source of the vitamin C in some of the vitamin tablets available in stores.

HOW TO SPOT

Size: Bushes, 3 to 5 feet (0.9 to 1.5 m) tall and wide

Habitat: Bright open ground, often on beaches

Fruit: 0.5 to 1.5 inches (1.3 to 3.8 cm) wide

Leaves: Compound, 3 to 6 inches (7.6 to 15.2 cm) long

Range: Alaska, Washington State, and northeastern North America

BIG SALTBUSH *(ATRIPLEX LENTIFORMIS)*

These dryland shrubs make green highlights against the dry, brown soils where they grow. In the spring, they produce clusters of tiny green flowers. Big saltbush plants have a trick for absorbing water from the dry, salty soils where they live, putting salt out onto their gray-green leaf surfaces. The leaves then have a white coating on them. These plants come from the goosefoot family and have similar leaves, which are lobed so they look like the feet of geese.

HOW TO SPOT

Size: Bushes, up to 30 feet (9.1 m) tall

Habitat: Sandy and rocky soils along roads, forest edges, shores

Leaves: Up to 2 inches (5.1 cm) long

Range: Western United States

BROADLEAF PLANTAIN

(PLANTAGO MAJOR)

This native plant of Europe is easy to find in lawns and along roadsides. It is pollinated by the wind. In summer, the tiny greenish-yellow flowers bloom on spikes that are 2 to 6 inches (5.1 to 15.2 cm) long. Each perennial plant can produce up to 20,000 seeds at a time. The oval leaves are excellent in salads, adding flavors of pepper and nuts. They can also be steamed like spinach and mixed with butter and cheese. It makes a great source of edible greens since it is common in North America.

HOW TO SPOT

Size: Flat rose-shaped groups of leaves 6 to 12 inches (15.2 to 30.5 cm) wide

Habitat: Moist, fertile soils in full sun

Leaves: 2 to 8 inches (5.1 to 20.3 cm) long; 1.5 to 3.5 inches (3.8 to 8.9 cm) wide

Range: United States and Canada

BULL THISTLE *(CIRSIUM VULGARE)*

This prickly cousin of lettuce and daisies grows for two years. The seed germinates and makes a circle, or rosette, of leaves on the soil surface in the first year. In the second year, the pinkish-purple flower spike appears in spring and summer. The seeds are fuzzy like those of a dandelion and float away on the wind. Small birds love them, making these seeds an important part of some birdseed mixes. Peeled, the young flower stems are juicy eaten raw or steamed.

HOW TO SPOT

Size: 3 to 5 feet (0.9 to 1.5 m) tall, with most leaves at the base
Habitat: Pastures, roadsides, ditches
Leaves: 8 to 24 inches (20.3 to 61 cm) long
Range: United States and Canada

CATCHWEED BEDSTRAW

(GALIUM APARINE)

Catchweed bedstraw provides a fun addition to salads or cooked greens when its leaves are used. The small, hooked hairs on its leaves and stems make them stick to each other like pieces of Velcro. These leaves grow in rings of six to eight around the stem. This annual plant makes star-shaped, white flowers that bloom in groups of two or three, growing out from along the stem in the spring. Like other bedstraw species, this one smells sweet when crushed.

HOW TO SPOT

Size: Along the ground, stems grow up to 6 feet (1.8 m) long and up to 6 inches (15.2 cm) high

Habitat: Moist, rich soils near forests

Leaves: 0.8 to 3.5 inches (2 to 8.9 cm) long

Range: United States and Canada

CATTAIL *(TYPHA LATIFOLIA)*

With edible young leaves—juicy when used raw—and edible nutty-flavored pollen, cattail is a very nutritious plant. It is a tall perennial plant. The rhizomes, when removed from the mud, can be used in place of potatoes because they are also so rich in starch. This was a favorite food of American Indians. The flower spikes, made of tiny brown flowers, can be used as torches. These spikes are 3 to 6 inches (7.6 to 15.2 cm) long, with female flowers clustered above male flowers.

HOW TO SPOT

Size: 5 to 10 feet (1.5 to 3 m) tall, almost all of that leaves
Habitat: Wetlands such as ditches, edges of ponds
Leaves: 0.8 to 1.5 inches (2 to 3.8 cm) wide; 5 to 10 feet (1.5 to 3 m) long
Range: United States and Canada (except Nunavut and Northern Territory)

CHICKWEED *(STELLARIA MEDIA)*

Appearing in spring as one of the first new green plants, chickweed can be eaten raw. It is a juicy part of salads. It can also be cooked, the way spinach is cooked. This annual plant has small oval leaves. Chickweed forms rounded mounds of greenery. The springtime flowers look like little white stars against the leaves, giving it the name *Stellaria*, meaning "star."

HOW TO SPOT

Size: 4 to 20 inches (10.2 to 50.8 cm) tall; 4 to 12 inches (10.2 to 30.5 cm) wide

Habitat: Cleared land and grassy areas, such as lawns and roadsides

Leaves: 0.3 to 1 inch (0.8 to 2.5 cm) long; 0.1 to 0.4 inches (0.3 to 1 cm) wide

Range: United States and Canada

FUN FACT

Chickweed leaves have a hydathode, or drip tip, at the end of each leaf. This is a special opening to allow excess water to drip out of the plant to prevent damage.

COMMON HORSETAIL

(EQUISETUM ARVENSE)

Horsetails look like the tails of horses. The main stems of this perennial have fine, hair-like branches. These plants were around when dinosaurs roamed Earth and are still here. This plant does not have flowers, but in spring, white cones form on white stems to make spores to make new plants. Various species of horsetails can be found on six continents. The young stems of this species can be cooked and eaten, providing lots of vitamins A, E, and C.

FUN FACT

Horsetails, including this species, are also called scouring rushes. This is because their stems contain silica, which are basically little pieces of glass. They can be used to scour pots and pans when camping.

HOW TO SPOT

Size: Stems 4 to 36 inches (10.2 to 91.4 cm) tall
Habitat: Wet ground, along streams and railroad tracks
Leaves: None, but thin branch stems take their place, 0.1 inch (0.3 cm) wide and 3 inches (7.6 cm) long
Range: United States (except Louisiana and Florida) and Canada

COMMON YELLOW WOOD SORREL

(OXALIS STRICTA)

This annual plant appears in spring. Its leaves have three heart-shaped leaflets. These leaves can fold up at night. The fruits are small, dry, and five-sided. The seeds are spread explosively: as the fruit dries, it squeezes the round seeds until they shoot up to 13 feet (4 m) away from the parent plant. The leaves, along with the yellow flowers that bloom in spring/summer, add a tart taste to salads. This tartness comes from the oxalic acid that they contain. But do not eat in high quantities; enjoy just a handful.

HOW TO SPOT

Size: Stems up to 9 inches (22.9 cm) tall
Habitat: Moist, usually sandy, soils, often in partial shade
Leaves: Compound, up to 0.8 inches (2 cm) wide
Range: United States (except California, Oregon, Nevada, and Utah) and Canada

CRESTED WOOD FERN

(DRYOPTERIS CRISTATA)

Each spring, this perennial produces large, deeply lobed leaves, called fronds. They grow in moist woods and wetlands. The young leaves are called fiddleheads. Fiddleheads are popular springtime vegetables fried in butter. It has no flowers, but in summer, spores are made in red-brown half circles under some leaves. Before the time of grocery stores, fiddleheads were a key food in springtime when the vegetable garden had not yet produced anything to eat.

HOW TO SPOT

Size: 1 to 3 feet (0.3 to 0.9 m) tall
Habitat: Wetlands and moist woods
Leaves: Compound, 1 to 3 feet (0.3 to 0.9 m) long
Range: United States (Washington State to Maine, south to Missouri, east to North Carolina, plus Tennessee and Georgia) and Canada

CURLY DOCK *(RUMEX CRISPUS)*

Curly dock is a perennial plant, which means it grows from year to year. It lives in wet soils. The large, strap-like leaves shade out smaller plants. These leaves are colored green to bronze. They should be cooked because eating them raw can cause health problems. They are used like spinach. In summer, yellow-green flowers appear in clusters along a tall spike. The red-brown, scratchy fruits are not much larger than seeds. This plant is related to buckwheat.

HOW TO SPOT

Size: Rosette of leaves up to 6 inches (15.2 cm) tall; flower spike up to 5 feet (1.5 m) tall

Habitat: Fields and roadsides, especially in wet soils

Leaves: 5.5 to 12 inches (14 to 30.5 cm) long; 2 to 3 inches (5.1 to 7.6 cm) wide

Range: United States and Canada (except Nunavut)

DANDELION *(TARAXACUM OFFICINALE)*

Dandelions are short lived-perennials. They get their name from the English version of the Italian name, *dente de leone*, meaning "lion's teeth." This name is based on their yellow flowers—yellow like a lion—and their wavy or toothed leaf edges. Cousins of lettuce, a dandelion has leaves that can be eaten fresh in salads or cooked like spinach. Their seeds have a parachute-like pappus, which allows the seeds to float away on the wind.

FUN FACT

Dandelions are considered weeds in North America—unwanted plants in our lawns and gardens. But they are popular elsewhere. In Italy, they have special varieties for use in cooking.

HOW TO SPOT

Size: 1 inch (2.5 cm) tall, but flowers and stems can be up to 28 inches (71.1 cm) tall; 2 to 16 inches (5.1 to 40.6 cm) wide

Habitat: Lawns, pastures, roadsides

Leaves: 2 to 18 inches (5.1 to 45.7 cm) long

Range: United States and Canada

FALSE SOLOMON'S SEAL

(MAIANTHEMUM RACEMOSUM)

This perennial woodland species grows in the understory, the plants below tall trees, in woodlands all over North America. Each stem has 5 to 15 shiny, light green, lance-shaped leaves pointing off to its sides. They prefer moist soils and are found with many other related plants from the lily family. In the spring, clusters of white flowers bloom. The young shoots can be eaten raw, or they can be steamed and then drizzled with salt and butter. Their flavor is like that of asparagus, which is eaten similarly.

HOW TO SPOT

Size: 1.7 to 3 feet (0.5 to 0.9 m) tall
Habitat: Moist woodlands with rich soil
Leaves: 3 to 6 inches (7.6 to 15.2 cm) long; 2 inches (5.1 cm) wide
Range: Continental United States and Canada (except Nunavut and Yukon)

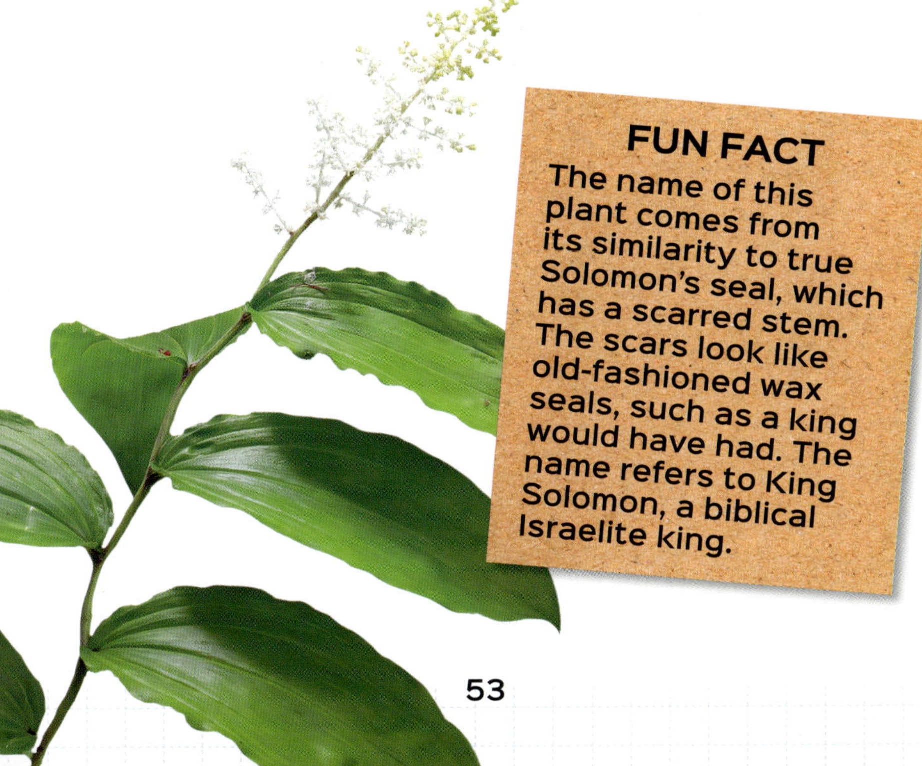

FUN FACT

The name of this plant comes from its similarity to true Solomon's seal, which has a scarred stem. The scars look like old-fashioned wax seals, such as a king would have had. The name refers to King Solomon, a biblical Israelite king.

GOOSEFOOT/LAMB'S QUARTERS

(CHENOPODIUM ALBUM)

Goosefoot stands tall, with many gray-green leaves on its branched stems. It contains large amounts of protein in its edible leaves and seeds, which is unusual for a green. This made it a favorite food of ancient American Indians. Eat the young leaves raw or sauté them. These annual plants often grow as weeds in gardens, starting as small circles of leaves. Each leaf is the shape of a goose's foot. In the summer, the plant's tiny gray-green flowers bloom along a flower stalk that is 4 to 16 inches (10.2 to 40.6 cm) tall.

FUN FACT

Goosefoot is a relative of quinoa, which can be found in the grocery store. Many American Indian groups grew quinoa for its seeds, cooked by boiling them until their white roots pop out of the seeds. Toss with oil or butter, add salt, and enjoy their nutty taste.

HOW TO SPOT

Size: 4 to 78 inches (10.2 to 198.1 cm) tall

Habitat: Cleared ground such as roadsides, lawns, and pastures

Leaves: 1 to 5 inches (2.5 to 12.7 cm) long; 1.1 to 1.4 inches (2.8 to 3.6 cm) wide

Range: United States and Canada

GREENBRIER *(SMILAX ROTUNDIFOLIA)*

Greenbrier vines use their long thorns to climb and scramble over rocks, fences, and other plants, often in the shade. The curved, bright green stems carry rounded, shiny leaves. The springtime clusters of greenish-white flowers are followed by dark blue-black berries. The young stems can be cooked and eaten, tasting like a combination of spinach and asparagus. It is often found near other vines, such as wild grapes. Its berries are also edible, used for jams and jellies or eaten fresh.

HOW TO SPOT

Size: Vines up to 20 feet (6.1 m) long
Habitat: Roadsides, forest clearings, thickets
Leaves: 2 to 5 inches (5.1 to 12.7 cm) wide
Range: Eastern North America from Texas to Ontario, Canada

HENBIT *(LAMIUM AMPLEXICAULE)*

In springtime, Midwestern farm fields, not yet planted with crops, turn pinkish purple with the flowers of this annual plant. Thousands of plants stretch across the landscape. Each plant is short, with rounded, paired leaves on square stems. The plants appear in large groups, year after year. They smell musty and minty, a relative of peppermint and spearmint. The leaves and stems are edible raw or after cooking, and they can also be dried and crushed for tea.

HOW TO SPOT

Size: 4 to 16 inches (10.2 to 40.6 cm) tall
Habitat: Cleared ground, such as farm fields or roadsides
Leaves: 0.8 to 1.2 inches (2 to 3 cm) wide
Range: United States and Canada (except Nunavut and the Northern Territory)

LADY'S THUMB *(POLYGONUM PERSICARIA)*

Lady's thumb is a common annual garden weed that also grows in any moist, open site. It is easiest to spot when in bloom. The pink flower spikes that are 1.5 inches (3.8 cm) tall stand out from surrounding plants in summer. They grow on the ends of the long, thin stems that arch toward the ground, pulled down by the many eye-shaped leaves that have sharp tips. It is eaten raw or cooked. The nutritious seeds can be ground into flour.

HOW TO SPOT

Size: Up to 3 feet (0.9 m) tall

Habitat: Rich moist soil in woods and on roadsides

Leaves: 2 to 6 inches (5.1 to 15.2 cm) long; 1.5 inches (3.8 cm) wide

Range: United States and Canada

MARSHMALLOW *(ALTHAEA OFFICINALIS)*

The flowers and lobed leaves of marshmallow are delicious in salads or sprinkled on other food. These perennial plants grow near water. The summertime bell-like, pink flowers are often the first thing spotted. Two close relatives of this plant are cotton, the kind used to make cloth, and okra, the vegetable used in soups and stews. Marshmallow is often grown in flower gardens, where there are kinds with white or red flowers. The roots were used to make the first marshmallow candies.

FUN FACT

The original candies called marshmallows were made with the marshmallow plant! Sugar compounds can be cooked out of the roots to make the sticky part of the marshmallow, which is then sweetened.

HOW TO SPOT

Size: Up to 6 feet (1.8 m) tall

Habitat: Wet ground, often in marshes or along ponds and lakes

Leaves: Up to 4 inches (10.2 cm) long; 3 inches (7.6 cm) wide

Range: United States (Maine to Virginia, Nebraska, Arkansas, Kentucky, and Ohio) and Canada (Ontario and Quebec)

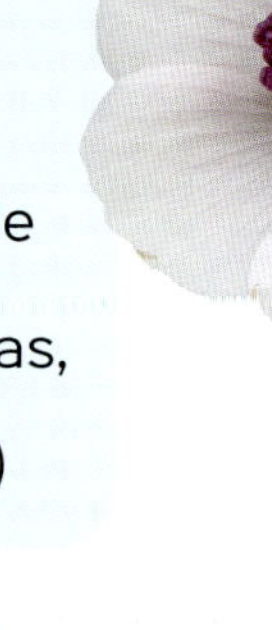

MINER'S LETTUCE

(CLAYTONIA PERFOLIATA)

Miner's lettuce is a wonderful winter and spring annual green for fresh eating. Its scientific species name comes from the fact that the small white, star-shaped flowers poke through two small, fused leaves in winter and spring. The flowers look like they break through this leaf—*perfoliata* means "poked-through leaf." This plant was commonly grown in gardens because it produced fresh vegetable material to eat earlier than most other crop plants.

HOW TO SPOT

Size: 0.4 to 12 inches (1 to 30.5 cm) tall

Habitat: Open ground to mixed forests in moist ground

Leaves: 6 to 12 inches (15.2 to 30.5 cm) long, including the stalk; up to 3.5 inches (8.9 cm) wide

Range: United States (Alaska, Washington State to California, east to Montana and New Mexico, Missouri, Georgia, and New Hampshire) and Canada (British Columbia)

MUGWORT *(ARTEMISIA VULGARIS)*

Mugwort is a perennial weed with jagged leaves that spreads by underground rhizomes. In summer, groups of tiny yellow-brown flowers bloom along a spike. The leaves are long, hairy, gray-green, and sharply divided into many small lobes. Mugwort is used as an herb in cooking. It has a strong flavor and odor, including some bitterness. Another name for mugwort is wormwood.

HOW TO SPOT

Size: 3 to 6 feet (0.9 to 1.8 m)

Habitat: Cleared areas with full sun, like roadsides and edges of woods

Leaves: 2 to 4 inches (5.1 to 10.2 cm) long; 2.5 inches (6.4 cm) wide

Range: United States (Minnesota to Louisiana and eastward, Washington State to Montana, south to California and Arizona) and Canada

FUN FACT

There are candies in Europe flavored using mugwort and other herbs.

PENNYWORT *(HYDROCOTYLE UMBELLATA)*

Pennywort has a strong, pleasant smell that reminds people of parsley and carrot leaves. Its bright green stems crawl along the ground, throwing up many round, lobed leaves. Tiny white clusters of flowers bloom in spring through autumn. Stems, leaves, and roots can be eaten fresh for the flavor they add to other dishes, similar to how cooks use parsley or dill.

FUN FACT

Pennywort is an easy plant to grow as a houseplant. Save a piece of stem with a few leaves. Put it in a pot with some soil and keep the soil wet. Keep it in a sunny window.

HOW TO SPOT

Size: Up to 8 inches (20.3 cm) tall, with creeping stems; 2 feet (0.6 m) long

Habitat: Wet ground and in shallow fresh water

Leaves: 0.2 to 3 inches (0.5 to 7.6 cm) wide

Range: United States (Oregon to California and Minnesota, Texas to Virginia and south, Indiana to Michigan, east to Delaware) and Canada (Nova Scotia)

PURSLANE *(PORTULACA OLERACEA)*

Purslane has leaves that are swollen with water, called succulent. These thick oval leaves are wider near the tip. They are edible, along with the stems and flowers that form in summer and autumn. The stems are round, creeping over the soil, tipped with the yellow flowers. They all add some tartness due to the safe chemical oxaloacetate in their cells. They can be used to flavor dishes because of that chemical, which they have because of the special kind of photosynthesis that they do.

HOW TO SPOT

Size: Up to 16 inches (40.6 cm) tall, spreading over the ground

Habitat: Many different habitats, but often in poor, dry soils

Leaves: 0.8 to 2 inches (2 to 5.1 cm) long; 0.2 to 0.8 inches (0.5 to 2 cm) wide

Range: United States and southern Canada

FUN FACT

Purslane is special because of the three kinds of photosynthesis it performs; it is the only plant that can do all three. It switches based on how much water is available.

RED MAIDS *(CALANDRINIA CILIATA)*

This annual plant has fleshy, tart leaves. The leaves are shaped like eyes, on stems that stand straight up from a circle of leaves on the ground. The flowers are extremely deep pink or red and easy to spot. It contains a chemical called oxalic acid, just like spinach. Red maid leaves should be cooked and drained before eating. The beautiful flowers only open if the day is sunny.

HOW TO SPOT

Size: 1 to 16 inches (2.5 to 40.6 cm) tall

Habitat: Grasslands and fields

Leaves: 0.4 to 4 inches (1 to 10.2 cm) long

Range: Western United States and Canada (British Columbia)

SHEPHERD'S PURSE

(CAPSELLA BURSA-PASTORIS)

Shepherd's purse comes from the mustard family. Its white flowers are cross-shaped and bloom in spring. The flowers and lobed leaves, which are great in salads, have a spicy, pepper flavor. The name of this plant comes from the fact that the seed pod looks like an old-fashioned coin purse. When the pod is broken open, the seeds look like small, round gold coins. This was the shepherd's purse and gold coins. Shepherd's purse is annual to biennial.

HOW TO SPOT

Size: A ring of leaves in the ground, about 3 to 6 inches (7.6 to 15.2 cm) wide; flower stems 8 to 18 inches (20.3 to 45.7 cm) tall

Habitat: Cleared areas, roadsides, farm fields

Leaves: 3 to 6 inches (7.6 to 15.2 cm) long

Range: United States and Canada

SMOOTH PIGWEED

(AMARANTHUS RETROFLEXUS)

This is one of several annual pigweed species found in North America. The leaves are rich in protein, which is true for all plants in the amaranth family. The tiny green flowers grow in spikes up to 4 inches (10.2 cm) long, appearing in summer. The flower spikes have a characteristic rough appearance. The leaves have many small hairs that you can feel. It also contains minerals needed by the human body, such as calcium, iron, and phosphorous. Cook and rinse the leaves before eating to reduce oxalic acid and nitrates.

HOW TO SPOT

Size: Up to 10 feet (3 m) tall
Habitat: Roadsides, farm fields, other cleared areas
Leaves: Up to 6 inches (15.2 cm) long
Range: United States and Canada

FUN FACT

Pigweeds get their name from the fact that they often grow where pigs have been fenced in.

SPIDERWORT *(TRADESCANTIA VIRGINIANA)*

Spiderwort grows along low, wet spots in eastern North America. Wild plants have purple-blue flowers, but cultivated plants may have other flower colors. The straight stems with round sides have triangular leaves that stick straight out. The leaves of this perennial are dark green and covered with soft hairs. The stems are edible, but the leaves are the most commonly eaten part. They are often used fresh in salads. The flowers can also be added to salads as a colorful accent.

HOW TO SPOT

Size: 2 to 3 feet (0.6 to 0.9 m), often leaning

Habitat: Wet, low ground with bright sunshine

Leaves: Up to 7 inches (17.8 cm) long; 1 inch (2.5 cm) wide

Range: Eastern United States, California, and Canada (Ontario)

FUN FACT

The flowers of spiderworts are colored by pigments that are pH sensitive and react to acids and bases. Crush a few flowers on a white plate. A little white vinegar turns them pink. A little baking soda turns them dark blue or even green! Observe and then discard the flowers.

WATERCRESS *(NASTURTIUM OFFICINALE)*

Watercress has rounded green leaves and fleshy white roots. This entire perennial plant makes dense mats along the edges of flowing streams. Stems run along the ground, with circles of many leaves. It flowers during all seasons, with white clusters of flowers opening a few at a time. Watercress floats because its stems and roots contain air spaces, life jackets to make it float. The leaves include many oval leaflets per leaf. Its spicy flavor is characteristic of plants in the mustard family.

FUN FACT

People in England enjoy watercress sandwiches. You can make them too. Spread cream cheese onto the bread and top with clean watercress leaves and thick slices of cucumber and any other cheese that you like. Add a little salt and pepper and enjoy.

HOW TO SPOT

Size: Plants extend from 1 to 10 feet (0.3 to 3 m) along streams

Habitat: Flowing streams, along the edge

Leaves: 1 to 6 inches (2.5 to 15.2 cm) long; about 1 inch (2.5 cm) wide

Range: United States (except North Dakota) and southern Canada

WHITE CLOVER *(TRIFOLIUM REPENS)*

White clover is an amazing perennial plant from the bean family. Its stem creeps along the ground, forming mats of plants. It makes leaves that each have three rounded leaflets with a white V shape. The flowers are white, in clusters called heads, 0.6 to 0.8 inches (1.5 to 2 cm) wide. It can pull its own fertilizer from the air with the help of bacteria. It is highly nutritious, with sweet-tasting flowers and delicious leaves for fresh eating. The nectar can also be sucked from individual flowers for a quick treat.

HOW TO SPOT

Size: Up to 6 inches (15.2 cm) tall

Habitat: Open grasslands and fields, full sun with high moisture

Leaves: Compound, up to 1.5 inches (3.8 cm) wide

Range: United States and Canada

WILD LETTUCE *(LACTUCA VIROSA)*

This biennial is a close cousin of garden lettuce. In summer, the plant makes 1-inch (2.5 cm) yellow flowers on tall stems. The leaves are deeply lobed, looking like the ends of spears. They stand upright in a ring. Like garden lettuce, there is some bitter taste. The bitter flavor is due to latex, a natural rubber made by the plant.

HOW TO SPOT

Size: Up to 6.7 feet (2 m) tall when in flower

Habitat: Open ground, such as roadsides, fields, edges of woods

Leaves: 3 to 10 inches (7.6 to 25.4 cm) long; 1 to 4 inches (2.5 to 10.2 cm) wide

Range: United States (Alabama, California, Iowa, and the District of Columbia) and Canada (Alberta)

CALIFORNIA WHITE SAGE

(SALVIA APIANA)

California white sage has massed oval leaves that are long, hairy, and gray-green. They have wavy edges and form a rounded mound, from which the spikes of flowers emerge in summer. The leaves have a savory flavor and are used to season meat and baked goods, like culinary sage available at the grocery store. It is also used in stews and soups for the same reason. This perennial has small, white flowers that bloom in spring and summer. These flowers are rich in sugary nectar and loved by bees. That leads to part of its scientific name, *apiana*, which refers to those honey bees.

HOW TO SPOT

Size: 4 to 5 feet (1.2 to 1.5 m) tall; 4 feet (1.2 m) wide
Habitat: Dry open sites with full sun
Leaves: 3 to 4 inches (7.6 to 10.2 cm) long
Range: Southern California to Baja California

MUCILAGE AND COOKING

Mucilage is a sticky chemical made of sugar in many plants. It makes foods thick. We often like that in soups and stews, so we add certain plants to our food to make the texture thicker.

DOWNY WOOD MINT *(BLEPHILIA CILIATA)*

Downy wood mint grows in drier locations than peppermint or spearmint and has a milder, minty scent. The straight stems of this perennial carry paired oval leaves. The summer flowers are up to 1 inch (2.5 cm) long, with fringed petals. The natural oils in the leaves also protect the plant from insects that would like to eat its leaves. The oils taste bad to insects. So insects leave the plants alone. The raw leaves can be used in salads or on other foods.

HOW TO SPOT

Size: 16 to 32 inches (40.6 to 81.3 cm) tall

Habitat: Dry sites in woodlands and open spaces like roadsides and fields

Leaves: Up to 3.5 inches (8.9 cm) long; 1.5 inches (3.8 cm) wide

Range: Eastern half of the United States (except Florida) and Canada (Ontario)

LEMON VERBENA *(ALOYSIA CITRIODORA)*

Lemon verbena is a perennial plant that has been introduced to North America from South America. It cannot survive freezing, though it can resprout from underground after light frost. Its leaves smell strongly of lemon and can be used to make flavorings and herbal teas. The species name *citriodora* means "citrus smelling," with lemon being a kind of citrus. These small trees are round in shape, with many medium-green, pointed leaves. The branched clusters of purple or white flowers appear in summer.

FUN FACT

There is a drink from South America flavored using an extract from lemon verbena. It is called Inca Kola, named after the ancient Inca natives, and it is produced in Peru, the center of the ancient Inca Empire.

HOW TO SPOT

Size: 7 to 10 feet (2.1 to 3 m) tall
Habitat: Full sun, moist rich soils in areas with little or no frost
Leaves: 3 inches (7.6 cm) long
Range: United States (California, Georgia, and North Carolina)

OXEYE DAISY *(LEUCANTHEMUM VULGARE)*

Oxeye daisies face the sun with their flowers poking up among other meadow plants. Their leaves are deeply lobed from stems along the ground. The white flowers have yellow centers. They bloom on long stems and are about 1 to 3 inches (2.5 to 7.6 cm) wide. The leaves and flowers add savory flavor to salads or other raw dishes, such as sandwiches. They can also be used as herbs for soups and stews. To have less bitter flavor, use younger parts.

HOW TO SPOT

Size: Up to 30 inches (76.2 cm) tall

Habitat: Open fields, meadows, roadsides, with full sun and moist soil

Leaves: 0.2 to 6 inches (0.5 to 15.2 cm) long

Range: United States and Canada (except Nova Scotia and Newfoundland)

PEPPERMINT *(MENTHA X PIPERITA)*

Peppermint is a perennial hybrid of two other mint species, and, like them, loves wet places. The stems come straight up from the ground and make oval, dark green leaves. The flowers are purple, about 0.3 inches (0.8 cm) long, in summer and autumn. Peppermint easily grows new roots on pieces of stem to make new plants. The leaves have oils that give them its distinct scent. The leaves, stems, and flowers can be dried and used to make teas. They can also be eaten fresh.

HOW TO SPOT

Size: 12 to 36 inches (30.5 to 91.4 cm) tall

Habitat: Moist to wet soils

Leaves: 1.5 to 3.5 inches (3.8 to 8.9 cm) long; 0.6 to 1.5 inches (1.5 to 3.8 cm) wide

Range: United States (except central states) and most of Canada

FUN FACT

Peppermint gets its flavor from oils held in oil glands. These are found in tiny round structures on the leaves. When you rub the leaf, you break the structures and release the oils.

PINEAPPLE WEED

(MATRICARIA DISCOIDEA)

Pineapple weed is a perennial that is also called wild chamomile. It is a member of the daisy family and tastes like pineapple. Its stems are upright, with many leaves that look like feathers because they are so deeply divided. The yellow-green flowers are dome-shaped with small white petals. Its leaves and flowers go well in salads or just eaten on their own. Mosquitoes hate the smell of this plant, so hang bunches of it to drive away those annoying insects.

HOW TO SPOT

Size: 2 to 16 inches (5.1 to 40.6 cm) tall

Habitat: Meadows and roadsides with full sun, lots of moisture

Leaves: 0.5 to 2 inches (1.3 to 5.1 cm) long

Range: United States (except Florida to South Carolina) and western and east-central Canada

PRICKLY ASH *(ZANTHOXYLUM AMERICANUM)*

This native tree grows in Eastern woodlands, producing clusters of small, red, dry, round fruits on its thorny branches. The medium-green compound leaves look like fern leaves. They have 5 to 11 leaflets. The large clusters of spring flowers are a mix of green and red and are 0.1 inches (0.3 cm) wide. They can be used as a substitute for pepper. People who are sensitive to Szechuan pepper should avoid eating this plant.

HOW TO SPOT

Size: Up to 33 feet (10.1 m) tall
Habitat: Moist woodlands, especially cooler locations
Fruit: 0.2 inches (0.5 cm) wide
Leaves: 4 to 12 inches (10.2 to 30.5 cm) long
Range: Eastern North America

QUICKWEED *(GALINSOGA PARVIFLORA)*

While the leaves and young stems of annual quickweed can be used as a vegetable, they are more often dried and used for teas. Quickweed comes from the daisy family, making it related to lettuce. It is also known as the gallant soldier plant. The flowers are small and have yellow centers and white petals. They grow in small clusters. The leaves are lobed, pointed ovals.

HOW TO SPOT

Size: Up to 30 inches (76.2 cm) tall

Habitat: Open places like roadsides and fields

Leaves: 1 to 3 inches (2.5 to 7.6 cm) long; 0.5 to 2 inches (1.3 to 5.1 cm) wide

Range: Most of the United States and Canada (Ontario to New Brunswick)

FUN FACT

Artichoke is a tasty flower bud from a giant thistle native to the Mediterranean and North Africa. If you like artichoke, you will love the flavor of quickweed, a great substitute for those big, expensive flower buds.

SASSAFRAS *(SASSAFRAS ALBIDUM)*

Perennial sassafras trees tower over many others with their deeply wrinkled bark. The young twigs are bright green, turning brown in patches until the young stems are fully hardened. Small yellow-green flowers appear in spring. The tree's mitten-shaped leaves turn fiery red and orange in the autumn after being dark green all summer. These leaves have a pungent, spicy odor when crushed. Sassafras was used historically to flavor root beer soda.

HOW TO SPOT

Size: 30 to 66 feet (9.1 to 20.1 m) tall

Habitat: Fertile, moist woodlands

Leaves: 4 to 6 inches (10.2 to 15.2 cm) long; 2 to 4 inches (5.1 to 10.2 cm) wide

Range: Eastern United States and Canada (Ontario)

FUN FACT

The young shoot tips and leaves of sassafras can be collected in spring while soft and flexible, then dried and crushed. In Louisiana, this is called filé powder, a staple in Cajun cooking, added to dishes such as soup and gumbo. This thickens those foods.

SPEARMINT *(MENTHA SPICATA)*

Spearmint's bright green leaves have a cool, spicy scent. This perennial member of the mint family has upright stems and round bright green leaves, like narrow ovals. It forms clumps of stems from white, underground rhizomes. In spring and summer, light purple flowers grow in spikes at the top of stems. These plants prefer moist soils and bright sunshine. The stem is square. Spearmint flavor makes it popular for teas and various dishes, especially desserts.

HOW TO SPOT

Size: 12 to 40 inches (30.5 to 101.6 cm) tall
Habitat: Moist, rich soils
Leaves: 2 to 3 inches (5.1 to 7.6 cm) long; 0.5 to 1 inch (1.3 to 2.5 cm) wide
Range: United States and Canada

SPICEBUSH *(LINDERA BENZOIN)*

Spicebush thrives in some shade in rich, moist soils. The leaves are pleasantly scented, with a mix of spice and citrus, on arching, thin brown stems. In heavy shade, the leaves are widely spaced. With more sun, the plant makes a rounded mound of leaves. In summer, yellow-green clusters of flowers form around the stem. Every autumn, loose clusters of oval, bright red berries jump into view against the bright yellow leaves. The pungent, spicy berries can be dried and ground, then used as a substitute for allspice in baking.

FUN FACT

Spicebush is a good substitute for allspice, a tropical spice. Allspice is the dried unripe berry of a tropical tree, and fairly expensive.

HOW TO SPOT

Size: 6 to 15 feet (1.8 to 4.6 m) tall bushes

Habitat: Woodlands with filtered sunlight or edges of woodlands

Fruit: 0.4 inches (1 cm) long

Leaves: 2 to 6 inches (5.1 to 15.2 cm) long; 0.8 to 2.5 inches (2 to 6.4 cm) wide

Range: Eastern United States and Canada (Ontario)

STAGHORN SUMAC *(RHUS TYPHINA)*

Staghorn sumac forms small trees in groups. Their compound leaves have toothed edges. The leaves turn a beautiful red in the autumn. The gray older stems are thin and flexible, carrying tiny clusters of white flowers in summer. Young stems can be eaten raw or cooked. The tiny, round, red, hairy seeds that form in clusters can be dried and ground into powder for use in Middle Eastern cooking. Their tart flavor can be used in sumac lemonade when sugar and water are added, or made into a delicious jelly.

HOW TO SPOT

Size: Up to 25 feet (7.6 m) tall and wide

Habitat: Fertile upland sites with full sun

Fruit: 0.25 inches (0.6 cm) wide

Leaves: 10 to 22 inches (25.4 to 55.9 cm) long

Range: Eastern half of United States (except Florida), Utah, South Dakota, Minnesota, and Nebraska, and eastern Canada

SWEETFERN *(COMPTONIA PEREGRINA)*

Sweetfern, not a true fern, has fern-like, lobed leaves. This perennial adds mild savory flavor to foods. Flowers bloom in the spring. The tiny nuts that form in clusters can be eaten raw or dried. Dry or moist, the lance-shaped, lobed leaves can be made into flavorful tea or used with the fruits to season meats, soups, and stews. There are separate male and female flowers, as in corn. Most other plants have one flower with both male and female parts.

HOW TO SPOT

Size: Shrubs to 5 feet (1.5 m) tall
Habitat: Dry, sandy soils, often near pine trees
Fruit: 0.3 to 0.8 inches (0.8 to 2 cm) wide
Leaves: 1.2 to 6 inches (3 to 15.2 cm) long; 0.1 to 1.2 inches (0.3 to 3 cm) wide
Range: Eastern North America

TEABERRY *(GAULTHERIA PROCUMBENS)*

Teaberry plants are often seen in cool northern forests in North America, creeping under the ground using buried stems, called rhizomes. They sit over the shiny, oval, evergreen leaves in spring or summer. The leaves and berries have a strong wintergreen scent. The berries are bright red and form in clusters. They can be eaten fresh or used in cooking. The leaves are a source for essential oils with this odor, used in flavoring candy and chewing gum.

HOW TO SPOT

Size: 4 to 8 inches (10.2 to 20.3 cm) tall
Habitat: Acidic soils in hardwood forests, partial sunlight
Fruit: 0.3 inches (0.8 cm) in diameter
Leaves: 0.8 to 2 inches (2 to 5.1 cm) long; 0.5 to 0.8 inches (1.3 to 2 cm) wide
Range: Eastern North America (except Florida)

WHITE SPRUCE *(PICEA GLAUCA)*

White spruce trees are evergreen trees. The needles can be made into a tasty, slightly sweet tea rich in vitamin C. The inner bark is edible and very nutritious. The young cones can also be processed for food. These cones, which make the seeds, are 1.3 to 2.5 inches (3.3 to 6.4 cm) long and 0.6 inches (1.5 cm) wide. Last, the resin can be chewed as a replacement for chewing gum. All parts of the tree are edible if processed properly and were key sources of winter food for American Indians.

HOW TO SPOT

Size: 50 to 100 feet (15.2 to 30.5 m)
Habitat: Wet, northern boreal forests
Leaves: Needles, 0.5 to 0.8 inches (1.3 to 2 cm) long
Range: Northern United States and Canada

WILD ANGELICA *(ANGELICA SYLVESTRIS)*

From the carrot family, this biennial grows in cold, northern soils. Its young stems, when peeled, are excellent when eaten fresh, tasting like licorice. The large, compound leaves can be eaten after boiling. The toothed leaves are found in a ring, with the flower stem standing straight up from them. The flowers grow in an umbrella-shaped group 4 to 9 inches (10.2 to 22.9 cm) wide. Be sure of the identification because the carrot family has many edible members and others that can be toxic to humans.

HOW TO SPOT

Size: Up to 8 feet (2.4 m) when in bloom
Habitat: Wide range of soils (sand to clay) and moisture levels (dry to full of water)
Leaves: 2 to 3 feet (0.6 to 0.9 m) long
Range: Eastern Canada

WILD CARAWAY *(CARUM CARVI)*

Wild caraway is the biennial wild version of the garden herb of the same name. The feathery leaves form a ring, the flowering stem growing up among them. In summer, the flowers bloom in umbrella-shaped groups 1 to 2.5 inches (2.5 to 6.4 cm) wide, each made of 20 flowers. The leaves are eaten fresh in salads or sandwiches or cooked in soups, stews, and teas. The seeds flavor many baked goods, including hot cross buns, and some cheeses. Even the roots can be harvested and cooked.

HOW TO SPOT

Size: Up to 2 feet (0.6 m) tall, when flowering

Habitat: Meadows, grasslands, roadsides, and ditches

Leaves: 8 to 12 inches (20.3 to 30.5 cm) long

Range: Northern and eastern United States and southern Canada

YARROW *(ACHILLEA MILLEFOLIUM)*

Yarrow is a perennial herb in the carrot family. While the leaves are eaten raw or cooked, most people think of using yarrow for teas. The teas make use of the sweetly fragrant flowers, which are white or pink in umbrella-shaped groups of 10 or more in the summer. The leaves grow in a ring on the ground. They are finely divided so they look like feathers. The oils in yarrow leaves drive away mosquitoes and other flying insects. These same oils can be extracted to make creams to soothe the skin.

HOW TO SPOT

Size: 0.6 to 3 feet (0.2 to 0.9 m) tall, when flowering

Habitat: Moist meadows, roadsides, other open sites with full sun

Leaves: 2 to 8 inches (5.1 to 20.3 cm) long

Range: United States and Canada

AMERICAN BEECH *(FAGUS GRANDIFOLIA)*

American beech trees are easy to spot in the eastern woods of North America from their large size and very smooth gray bark. The pointed leaves have prominent veins. In the fall, this perennial drops three-sided edible brown beech nuts. These come out of husks covered in thick, hair-like structures. These delicious nuts are rich in fat and protein, making them popular with animals as well as people. Young leaves can be eaten raw in salads or used to flavor cooked dishes, including soups.

HOW TO SPOT

Size: 50 to 120 feet (15.2 to 36.6 m)

Habitat: Rich soils, moist but well-drained uplands

Fruit: 0.5 to 1 inch (1.3 to 2.5 cm) long

Leaves: 2.5 to 5 inches (6.4 to 12.7 cm) long

Range: Eastern half of North America and Utah

AMERICAN FILBERT

(CORYLUS AMERICANA)

The American filbert is a small tree or large shrub. It is the first cousin of hazelnuts. It forms wide plants with many main stems growing from the base of the whole plant. The leaves are heart-shaped and toothed on their edges. The round, light brown nuts are produced in autumn. They have a large white circle at one end. They taste just like hazelnuts and grow on the ends of the long, flexible gray branches.

HOW TO SPOT

Size: 8 to 15 feet (2.4 to 4.6 m) tall
Habitat: Moist rich woodland soils
Fruit: Nuts, 0.4 to 0.8 inches (10 to 20 mm) wide
Leaves: 3.1 to 4.7 inches (7.9 to 11.9 cm) long
Range: Midwestern and eastern North America except Florida

FUN FACT

One of the best known uses of the European hazelnut is making a mix of ground hazelnut with chocolate. You can do the same with filberts. The main ingredients that you will need are the ground filberts, powdered sugar, and melted chocolate.

WHAT IS A NUT?

Nuts are dried fruits surrounded by a very hard shell. The shell has to be cracked for the seed inside to be eaten. Tree nuts, such as walnuts and pecans, are usually rich in fat. Many "nuts," such as peanuts, are not true nuts.

BLACK WALNUT *(JUGLANS NIGRA)*

The black walnut tree is a key species in eastern US forests, providing its sweet, fat-rich nuts for wildlife. The compound leaves of this tree are made of 15 to 23 leaflets. The round, green, bumpy nuts fall to the ground from the tall, dark brown trees with deeply cut bark. The nuts turn black after falling from the tree. The oil from the nuts can be used in cooking and in preserving wood. In spring, the sap can be tapped and collected to make sweet syrup.

HOW TO SPOT

Size: 70 to 130 feet (21.3 to 39.6 m) tall

Habitat: Rich, moist forest soils

Fruit: Nuts, 3 inches (7.6 cm) wide

Leaves: Compound, 1 to 2 feet (0.3 to 0.6 m) long

Range: Eastern and central North America

WALNUT INK

Boiling black walnut husks in water produces a brown ink that can be used with old-fashioned dip pens. The ink can be turned more blue-purple by adding rust from a rusty piece of metal.

COLORADO PINYON *(PINUS EDULIS)*

A favorite food of some American Indian tribes, the nutritious seeds of the perennial pinyon pine are produced each year in cones 1.3 to 2 inches (3.3 to 5.1 cm) long and wide at the end of flexible, brown branches. The scientific name of this species even means "edible pine." The nuts are both sweet and rich, due to their high fat content, including a large amount of heart-healthy oil.

FUN FACT

American Indian tribes worked together to harvest the pinyon pine nuts, which would be ready for harvest at one time and in large numbers. They even built special buildings to process and store this food. This staple food was crucial for the tribes' survival through winter's cold.

HOW TO SPOT

Size: 10 to 20 feet (3 to 6.1 m) tall
Habitat: Dry western forests, open and partly open areas
Fruit: Nuts, 0.4 to 0.6 inches (1 to 1.5 cm) long
Leaves: Needles, 1.1 to 2.1 inches (2.8 to 5.3 cm) long
Range: Southwestern United States

PECAN *(CARYA ILLINOINENSIS)*

Eastern forests in North America contain many species of hickory nuts, cousins of the black walnut. The best-known hickory, eaten around the world, is the pecan. The nuts from this tree are much longer than those of other hickories. They are sharply pointed at one end. The tall trees have gray-brown bark and compound leaves made of 9 to 17 leaflets. The nuts are brown when ripe. They can be eaten raw or roasted and are usually made into baked goods.

FUN FACT

All hickory nuts, such as pecans, are rich in healthy oils and have a sweet flavor. American Indians planted hickory trees in forests and relied on the nuts for winter foods, with families gathering many bushels of nuts each autumn.

HOW TO SPOT

Size: 65 to 130 feet (19.8 to 39.6 m) tall
Habitat: Rich, moist forest soils
Fruit: Nuts, 1.5 to 2.5 inches (3.8 to 6.4 cm)
Leaves: Compound, 4 to 8 inches (10.2 to 20.3 cm) long
Range: Southeastern and central United States and northern Mexico

PIGNUT HICKORY *(CARYA GLABRA)*

Pignut hickory trees have compound leaves made of five to seven leaflets. These trees produce light brown, round nuts with raised seams. These are some of the smaller hickory nuts and a large portion of the diet of some animals, such as chipmunks and gray squirrels. The nuts are sweet and rich in healthy oils. They can be roasted or eaten raw, added to salads, and baked into breads and pies.

HOW TO SPOT

Size: 50 to 60 feet (15.2 to 18.3 m) tall
Habitat: Rich, moist forest soils
Fruit: Nuts, 1.3 inches (3.3 cm) wide
Leaves: Compound, 8 to 12 inches (20.3 to 30.5 cm) long
Range: Eastern United States and Canada (Ontario)

TEPARY BEAN *(PHASEOLUS ACUTIFOLIUS)*

The annual tepary bean is native to dry areas of the US southwest as well as parts of Mexico. It is much more drought tolerant than the common bean available in markets, such as green beans. The tepary bean was turned into a farm crop by native tribes. Its long climbing vines have compound leaves and whitish-pink flowers 0.5 inch (1.3 cm) long and wide. The flowers are followed by pods that hold two to nine nutritious seeds. The beans can be eaten fresh or cooked like the common bean.

HOW TO SPOT

Size: 13 feet (4 m) long vines

Habitat: Desert and semidesert soils

Fruit: Pods, 1.3 to 3.5 inches (3.3 to 8.9 cm) long

Leaves: Compound, 4 inches (10.2 cm) long

Range: Southwestern United States and Mexico

WHITE OAK *(QUERCUS ALBA)*

The white oak tree can easily be found in eastern forests. Look for its deeply lobed leaves and the nuts on the ground near the tree's base in the autumn. These very large trees have medium brown bark. A large tree can produce up to several hundred pounds (more than 100 kg) of brown nuts. These acorns should be soaked in water to leech out the bitter tannins to improve flavor. They are eaten fresh, roasted for baked goods, or ground into flour.

FUN FACT

The white oak has a very important role in providing wood for furniture and building. Oak lumber is very hard and strong. Its beautiful pale color allows it to be stained a wide range of colors as well.

HOW TO SPOT

Size: 80 to 100 feet (24.4 to 30.5 m), occasionally up to 200 feet (61 m)
Habitat: Eastern woodlands with moist soils
Fruit: Nuts, 0.75 to 1 inch (1.9 to 2.5 cm) long
Leaves: 5 to 9 inches (12.7 to 22.9 cm) long
Range: Eastern North America

WILD BEAN *(PHASEOLUS POLYSTACHIOS)*

The wild bean is a close perennial relative of the common bean, *Phaseolus vulgaris*, which we find in markets and home gardens. The vine has compound leaves with three leaflets per leaf. The plants have bright pink flowers that are 0.1 inches (0.3 cm) long along the climbing vines. This bean has shorter pods with fewer beans but is used like common beans. The squarish black beans inside the pod are eaten fresh or cooked. Wild bean pods do not split open when they are fully mature, making them easier to harvest.

HOW TO SPOT

Size: 3 to 13 feet (0.9 to 4 m) tall as vines

Habitat: Woodlands and rocky areas such as cliffs and rocky slopes

Fruit: Pods, 1.1 to 2.4 inches (2.8 to 6.1 cm) long; 0.5 inches (1.3 cm) wide

Leaves: Compound, 3 inches (7.6 cm) long and wide

Range: Eastern United States

FUN FACT

The genus *Phaseolus* gives us many edible beans. Its species all come from the Americas and are rich in protein and minerals.

YELLOW LOTUS *(NELUMBO LUTEA)*

Yellow lotus thrives in cool, clean water. Some of this plant's large round leaves float on the surface while the others are held in the air. This perennial produces yellow flowers that are 7 to 11 inches (17.8 to 27.9 cm) wide, each with several dozen yellow petals. A cone-shaped, dry, brown pod has seeds sticking partway out of the top of this fruit. The swollen underwater stems, or tubers, are also edible. In addition, the leaves can be eaten fresh in salads. The flower petals can be dried and added to tea, often with green tea leaves.

HOW TO SPOT

Size: At most 1 to 2 feet (0.3 to 0.6 m) above the water
Habitat: Ponds and lakes with clean water, full sun
Fruit: Cone, up to 6 inches (15.2 cm) wide, with seeds
Leaves: 13 to 17 inches (33 to 43.2 cm) wide
Range: Eastern United States, Canada (Ontario), and parts of Mexico

CHICORY *(CICHORIUM INTYBUS)*

Chicory, with its beautiful blue to light purple summer flowers, grows in many wild places, as well as being cultivated. It starts as a ring of leaves that have small tooth-like extensions on the sides. They produce a straight, flowering stem in the second year of growth. In the wild, it grows among many other plants and is easy to spot along roads. Its long main root, or taproot, can be dried, roasted, and ground to replace coffee. Chicory leaves can be eaten in salads.

HOW TO SPOT

Size: 3 inches to 5 feet (7.6 cm to 1.5 m) tall, depending on whether it has been cut
Habitat: A variety of soils, from fertile to poor, with bright sunshine
Leaves: 1 to 8 inches (2.5 to 20.3 cm) long; 1 to 3 inches (2.5 to 7.6 cm) wide
Range: United States and southern Canada

CHUFA *(CYPERUS ESCULENTUS)*

Looking like grass plants, this perennial sedge grows widely with its triangular stems. It easily becomes a weed. It grows best where the soil is wet. Many sedges grow in North America, but only a few, including this one, make edible tubers underground. Tubers are underground swollen stems that contain nutrients. Tubers are usually good for people to eat. Potatoes are a great example. Chufa tubers are called nuts.

HOW TO SPOT

Size: Up to 3 feet (0.9 m) tall

Habitat: Prefers moist soils, but grows in a very wide range of habitats

Leaves: Up to 18 inches (45.7 cm) long

Range: United States and eastern and western Canada

CARBOHYDRATES IN TUBERS

Carbohydrates are made by putting sugars together to make very big molecules. Starch is one of these molecules, found in large amounts in rice, potatoes, and other tubers.

COMMON BURDOCK *(ARCTIUM MINUS)*

Common burdock stands out on the edge of moist woods, with its very large leaves that form a ring coming out of the ground. The tall flowering stem of this perennial bears 0.8-inch (2 cm) reddish-pink flowers with hooks on their outsides. The hooks catch clothing and fur like Velcro. While the leaves and leaf stalks can be eaten raw or cooked, when young, the main thing to eat are the roots. Roots are tender enough to eat until they are about one year old. They are washed, peeled, and boiled, the water changed, boiled again, and seasoned.

HOW TO SPOT

Size: Up to 6 feet (1.8 m) tall when in flower
Habitat: Open spaces such as roadsides ditches, the edge of woods, often in moist soils
Leaves: Up to 20 inches (50.8 cm) long
Range: United States (except Florida) and southern Canada

GARLIC ONION *(ALLIUM VINEALE)*

Garlic onion plants sprout each spring from 0.4- to 0.8-inch (1 to 2 cm) diameter bulbs underground. This perennial makes clusters of tall, hollow, tubular leaves. The bulbs are edible, along with the leaves and flowers. The pink or white clusters of flowers rarely produce seed. These flowers produce bulbils, tiny red bulbs at the top of the plant, that appear on the end of the flower stalk. The bulbils can be tossed by the wind to new growing locations. When cows eat these plants, their milk is garlic flavored.

HOW TO SPOT

Size: 12 to 48 inches (30.5 to 121.9 cm) tall when in bloom
Habitat: Open, sunny places like roadsides and farm fields
Leaves: 0.1 to 0.2 inches (0.3 to 0.5 cm) wide; 4 to 24 inches (10.2 to 61 cm) long
Range: West Coast and Eastern North America, and Canada (British Columbia)

GROUND NUT *(APIOS AMERICANA)*

Ground nut tubers were harvested by American Indians for their abundant nutrients, including calcium and iron. They contain many times the protein found in potatoes. The vines wander through other plants on the edges of woods. They have reddish-brown flowers about 0.3 inches (0.8 cm) wide, in spikes 3 to 5 inches (7.6 to 12.7 cm) long. Before eating, tubers should be cooked.

HOW TO SPOT

Size: Vines 3 to 20 feet (0.9 to 6 m) long
Habitat: Moist soils in full sun, climbing on taller plants
Leaves: Compound, 3 to 6 inches (7.6 to 15.2 cm) long
Range: Eastern United States and Canada

KUDZU *(PUERARIA MONTANA)*

Kudzu is a Japanese vine from the bean family. It was brought to the southern part of the United States to reduce soil loss. Kudzu can grow very fast, causing problems. It has compound leaves with three leaflets per leaf. However, it has edible roots, oval leaves, stem tips, and spikes of purple flowers in summer. The roots are dried, powdered, and used either for teas or for thickening soups and sauces. The other parts can be eaten fresh or cooked.

HOW TO SPOT

Size: Up to 100 feet (30.5 m) long, with up to 66 feet (20.1 m) of new growth per year

Habitat: Edges of woodlands and vertical surfaces where the vines can climb

Leaves: Compound, 2 to 8 inches (5.1 to 20.3 cm) long

Range: United States (except west-central states)

KUDZU ATE THE SOUTH

Kudzu was brought to the American South from Japan to save the soil. However, it grows out of control, covering houses and cars in a few weeks. That is why it is called "the vine that ate the South."

RAMPS *(ALLIUM TRICOCCUM)*

Ramps are mild, like an onion relative called leeks. Ramps grow in shady woods. They have wide, flat leaves that emerge each spring from underground bulbs. Medium green, they are followed by groups of white flowers that are 0.1 to 0.3 inches (0.3 to 0.8 cm) long and up to 1.5 inches (3.8 cm) wide. The leaves taste like a milder version of onions, similar to the garden plant called a shallot. Ramps grow slowly, so don't pick too many when harvesting.

HOW TO SPOT

Size: Up to 12 inches (30.5 cm) tall, in flower
Habitat: Part shade in forests
Leaves: 8 to 12 inches (20.3 to 30.5 cm) long
Range: Eastern North America

FUN FACT

Ramps have been picked too much in recent years when people learned how tasty they are. You can find information online, with help from an adult, on how to grow your own ramps.

WILD GINGER *(ASARUM CANADENSE)*

Wild ginger tastes a lot like ginger from the store, though it is not a close relative of true ginger. This plant appears in early spring. It has heart-shaped, hairy leaves. The root can be picked, peeled, and used in cooking, often candied. American Indians used wild ginger for many problems, including stomach issues. Do not eat too much of it to avoid kidney problems—the amount used for making things like gingerbread should be safe. Also, do not eat the poisonous leaves.

HOW TO SPOT

Size: 4 to 8 inches (10.2 to 20.3 cm) tall

Habitat: Moist woodlands with deep shade

Leaves: Up to 6 inches (15.2 cm) wide

Range: Eastern North America

BLADDER WRACK *(FUCUS VESICULOSUS)*

This seaweed is a brown alga, growing in the northern part of the Atlantic Ocean. It grows in shallow salt water. Air-filled bubbles, or vesicles, on its flat stems keep it floating in the water. The whole plant is greenish brown. The stems are partly flattened, looking like leaves of land plants. Like other seaweeds, it is rich in iodine and other minerals. It is used to make soups and stews. It is also used to make iodine pills.

HOW TO SPOT

Size: Up to 60 inches (152.4 cm) long, branched
Habitat: Shallow ocean water near the coast
Range: Eastern North American coast, from North Carolina to Newfoundland and Quebec, Canada

DULSE *(PALMARIA PALMATA)*

This red alga grows around the northern Atlantic Ocean, with its flat red stems acting like leaves for photosynthesis. It has been harvested for at least 1,500 years for use in cooking. It adds salt to food and can be removed after the food becomes salty enough. It also has carbohydrates, chemicals made of sugars, which make soups, stews, and sauces thicker. When it is cooked, those carbohydrates leave the seaweed and go into the soup or stew.

HOW TO SPOT

Size: Up to 20 inches (50.8 cm) long; 1 to 3 inches (2.5 to 7.6 cm) wide

Habitat: Ocean water, near the coast

Range: Eastern North American coast, from Pennsylvania to Newfoundland and Quebec, Canada

FUN FACT

Dulse is a snack food, not just an ingredient. If you go to a market in eastern Canada, you will find salty dried dulse next to the potato chips. It is eaten like chips, right out of a bag.

GLOSSARY

annual
A plant that grows for one season, then flowers and dies.

antioxidant
A chemical that protects cells from damage.

astringent
Contains chemicals that make the mouth pucker.

biennial
A plant that grows for one year and flowers the second year.

compound leaf
A leaf that is broken into several smaller leaflets.

flower
The part of a plant that makes seeds and fruits.

fruit
The covering over the seeds of a plant.

leaflets
Leaf-like structures that together make up a compound leaf.

perennial
A plant that grows for many years, flowering in the second and all other years.

rhizome
An underground stem, often thick and full of nutrients.

tart
Sour.

toothed
Having a jagged edge.

tuber
A rounded underground storage stem full of nutrients.

understory
The plants that grow under the cover of a forest's leaves.

TO LEARN MORE

FURTHER READINGS

Lyle, K. L. *The Complete Guide to Edible Wild Plants, Mushrooms, Fruits, and Nuts Finding, Identifying, and Cooking.* Falcon Guides, 2016.

Telander, Todd. *Edible Wild Plants: A Falcon Field Guide*. Falcon Guides, 2024.

US Department of the Army. *The Pocket Guide to Edible Wild Plants: How to Forage Safely and Responsibly*. Skyhorse, 2024.

ONLINE RESOURCES

To learn more about edible wild plants, please visit **abdobooklinks.com** or scan this QR code. These links are routinely monitored and updated to provide the most current information available.

PHOTO CREDITS

Cover Photos: step2626/E+/Getty Images, front (huckleberry); Gardens by Design/Shutterstock, front (wrinkled rose hips); Kabar/Shutterstock, front (wrinkled rose flower); vagabond54/Shutterstock, front (black huckleberry); Valentyn Volkov/Shutterstock, front (chicory); Olga S photography/Shutterstock, front (white oak); Zen Rial/Moment/Getty Images, front (maypop); DigiPub/Moment/Getty Images, front (beautyberry); veggie only/Shutterstock, front (strawberry tomato); Brian Woolman/Shutterstock, front (downy wood mint); New Africa/Shutterstock, front (trifoliate orange); Armastas/iStock/Getty Images, front (common horsetail); dadalia/Shutterstock, back (marshmallow); Gummy Bear/Shutterstock, back (American elderberry)

Interior Photos: Photoongraphy/Shutterstock, 1 (top left), 29 (left); Ruttawee Jai/Shutterstock, 1 (top right), 60 (top); Norman Posselt/fStop/Getty Images, 1 (center);William E. Fehr/Shutterstock, 1 (bottom left), 78; Malgorzata Wl/Shutterstock, 1 (bottom right); 98 (right); suttirat wiriyanon/Shutterstock, 2, 97 (right); Nancy J. Ondra/Shutterstock, 4 (left), 82 (bottom); dadalia/Shutterstock, 4 (right), 58 (bottom); Nikilev/Shutterstock, 5 (top left), 90 (right); Kabar/Shutterstock, 5 (top center), 41 (bottom); Ed Reschke/Photodisc/Getty Images, 5 (top right), 50 (right); Surawit K. Sakul/Shutterstock, 5 (bottom left), 79; Ed Reschke/Stone/Getty Images, 5 (bottom right), 55 (top), 84 (top), 112 (left); Donna Bollenbach/Shutterstock, 8, 66 (right); Brian Lasenby/Shutterstock, 9; Justus de Cuveland/imageBROKER/Getty Images, 10; Chase D'animulls/Shutterstock, 11 (top); Gummy Bear/Shutterstock, 11 (bottom); Olena Ruban/Moment/Getty Images, 12 (left); Anna_Pustynnikova/Shutterstock, 12 (right); photo by Pam Susemiehl/Moment/Getty Images, 13 (left); Jaylene Trotman/Shutterstock, 13 (right); Stephanie Frey/Shutterstock, 14 (left); Marinodenisenko/Shutterstock, 14 (right), 28, 76, 112 (top right); Barbara Smits/Shutterstock, 15; Golden Shark 2/Shutterstock, 16 (top), 21 (left); CampSmoke/Shutterstock, 16 (bottom); Federica Grassi/Moment/Getty Images, 17 (left); Nata Naumovec/Shutterstock, 17 (right); Marcia Straub/Moment/Getty Images, 18; Gerald Corsi/iStock/Getty Images, 19, 63 (left); Stelian Gavril/Shutterstock, 20 (left); Judy Gallagher/Flickr, 20 (right); Iuliia Bondar/Moment/Getty Images, 21 (right); MARCO CATULLO/Shutterstock, 22 (left); Michaela B/500px/Getty Images, 22 (right); GRADIENT BACKGROUND/Shutterstock, 23 (left); Jonas Vegele/Shutterstock, 23 (right); Aigul Minnibaeva/Shutterstock, 24 (left); Hasanov Mikayil/Shutterstock, 24 (right); Luis Alvaz/Wikimedia Commons, 25 (left); Jared Quentin/Shutterstock, 25 (right); Nadya So/Shutterstock, 26 (top); KWJPHOTOART/Shutterstock, 26 (bottom); Gerry Bishop/Shutterstock, 27; nnattalli/Shutterstock, 29 (right); Zen Rial/Moment/Getty Images, 30; Hajo Hajo/F1online/Getty Images, 31; Olena Lialina/iStock/Getty Images, 32 (left); John Farrell/500px/Getty Images, 32 (right), 112 (center); ForestSeasons/Shutterstock, 33 (top), 80 (right); Muriel Lasure/Shutterstock, 33 (bottom); e_rik/Shutterstock, 34 (left); EQRoy/Shutterstock, 34 (right); Iva Vagnerova/Shutterstock, 35 (left); imageBROKER/Helmut Meyer zur Capellen/Getty Images, 35 (right); Tatyana Mi/Shutterstock, 36 (left); Grigorii_Pisotckii/iStock/Getty Images, 36 (right); bergamont/iStock/Getty Images, 37 (top); Joe DiTomaso/Design Pics/Getty Images, 37 (bottom); Elisyah Harahap/Shutterstock, 38 (left); Randy Bjorklund/

Shutterstock, 38 (right); New Africa/Shutterstock, 39; Johner Images/Johner Images Royalty-Free/Getty Images, 40; Gardens by Design/Shutterstock, 41 (top); Jared Quentin/iStock/Getty Images, 42 (top); MuhammadAsif6/Shutterstock, 42 (bottom); medvezok/Shutterstock, 43 (left); Paul Starosta/Corbis/Getty Images, 43 (right); olko1975/Shutterstock, 44, 57; undefined undefined/iStock/Getty Images, 45 (left), 45 (right); krblokhin/iStock/Getty Images, 46 (left); Camptoloma/Shutterstock, 46 (right); Furiarossa/Shutterstock, 47 (top); Stefan Rotter/iStock/Getty Images, 47 (bottom); Orest Lyzhechka/iStock/Getty Images, 48 (left); aga7ta/Shutterstock, 48 (right); Rahma Riska/Shutterstock, 49; Steve Ansell/iNaturalist, 50 (left); Wirestock/iStock/Getty Images, 51 (left); MaryAnne Campbell/Shutterstock, 51 (right); Madeleine_Steinbach/iStock/Getty Images, 52 (top); milart/Shutterstock, 52 (bottom); Karel Bock/iStock/Getty Images, 53; simona pavan/Shutterstock, 54 (top); Enrique Díaz/7cero/Moment/Getty Images, 54 (bottom); Franklin Bonner, USFS (ret.), Bugwood.org/Forestry Images, 55 (bottom); TAMER YILMAZ/Shutterstock, 56; Kylbabka/Shutterstock, 58 (top); Martin Fowler/Shutterstock, 59; nancykennedy/iStock/Getty Images, 60 (bottom); Bowonpat Sakaew/Shutterstock, 61; ErikAgar/iStock/Getty Images, 62 (left); wasanajai/Shutterstock, 62 (right); Rix Pix Photography/Shutterstock, 63 (right); Lewis Pidoux/Shutterstock, 64; Noor Wahid/Shutterstock, 65; nickkurzenko/iStock/Getty Images, 66 (left); Ali Majdfar/Moment/Getty Images, 67; two K/Shutterstock, 68 (top); Tsekhmister/Shutterstock, 68 (bottom); Sinn P. Photography/Shutterstock, 69; Deborah Kunzie/Shutterstock, 70; Brian Woolman/Shutterstock, 71 (left), 102 (left); James St. John/Flickr, 71 (right); Mauro Rodrigues/Shutterstock, 72 (left); STUDIO GRAND WEB/Shutterstock, 72 (right); Frank Bienewald/LightRocket/Getty Images, 73 (top); Harry Rose/Flickr, 73 (bottom); Janisbija/Shutterstock, 74; Orest lyzhechka/Shutterstock, 75, 77; mizy/Shutterstock, 80 (left); Flower_Garden/Shutterstock, 81 (left); Ethan Jackson/500px/Getty Images, 81 (right); Megan Hansen/Flickr, 82 (top); Nahhana/Shutterstock, 83 (left), 112 (bottom right); Gabriela Beres/Shutterstock, 83 (right); skhoward/E+/Getty Images, 84 (bottom); Dsmile88/Shutterstock, 85 (left); DEA/E. MARTINI/De Agostini/Getty Images, 85 (right); Iker Zabaleta/Shutterstock, 86 (top); Dajra/Shutterstock, 86 (bottom); Mantonature/E+/Getty Images, 87 (left); SakSa/Shutterstock, 87 (right); Scisetti Alfio/Shutterstock, 88; Olga Aniven/Shutterstock, 89; Julia N/500px/Getty Images, 90 (left); Don Mammoser/Shutterstock, 91; Alf Ribeiro/Shutterstock, 92; R_Johnson/Shutterstock, 93; Tracey Slotta/USDA-NRCS PLANTS Database, 94 (top); Kendal Swart/Shutterstock, 94 (bottom); Olga S photography/Shutterstock, 95; Paul Rothrock/SEINet Portal Network, 96 (top); Fritzflohrreynolds/Wikimedia Commons, 96 (bottom); Liz Albro Photography/Shutterstock, 97 (left); NANCY AYUMI KUNIHIRO/Shutterstock, 98 (left); Doikanoy/Shutterstock, 99 (left); Nata Studio/Shutterstock, 99 (right); Mieszko9/Shutterstock, 100 (left); Denis Shitikoff/Shutterstock, 100 (right); MGn42/Shutterstock, 101; KOHUKU/Shutterstock, 102 (right); Jerry Whaley/Photographer's Choice RF/Getty Images, 103 (left); NNehring/E+/Getty Images, 103 (right); Karel Bock/Shutterstock, 104; Tim Masters/Shutterstock, 105 (top); japatino/Moment/Getty Images, 105 (bottom); Santiago Urquijo/Moment Open/Getty Images, 106; Voctir/Wikimedia Commons, 107

ABDOBOOKS.COM
Published by Abdo Reference, a division of ABDO, PO Box 398166, Minneapolis, Minnesota 55439.

Printed in China
102024
012025

Editor: Athena McGee
Series Designer: Colleen McLaren

Library of Congress Control Number: 2024938366
Publisher's Cataloging-in-Publication Data

Names: Darnowski, Douglas W., author.
Title: Edible wild plants / by Douglas W. Darnowski
Description: Minneapolis, Minnesota : Abdo Reference, 2025 | Series: North American field guides | Includes online resources and index.
Identifiers: ISBN 9781098296148 (lib. bdg.) | ISBN 9798384917144 (ebook)
Subjects: LCSH: Wild plants, Edible--Juvenile literature. | Edible weeds--Juvenile literature. | Wild plants as food--Juvenile literature. | Forage plants--Juvenile literature. | Ecological science--Juvenile literature.
Classification: DDC 581.6--dc23